Planning

a Wedding to Remember

THE PERFECT WEDDING PLANNER

Special Touches & Unique Ideas by BEVERLY CLARK

Book design by Studio R

Cover photo by Claudia Kunin

Illustrations by Karen Bell

Edited by Kathleen Peters

Personalized Wedding Bell by Maryann Cosgrove
To order bells, call (213) 270-3049

Lithographed in the U.S.A.
10 9 8 7 6 5 4 3 2 1

ISBN 0-934081-09-3

Published by Wilshire Publications
A division of Beverly Clark Collection
Distributor to gift and bridal trade
1120 Mark Avenue
Carpinteria, California 93013
Tel.: (805) 566-1425
Fax: (805) 566-1426

Distributor to the book trade:
Publishers Group West
4065 Hollis
Emeryville, California 94608
Tel.: (510) 658-3453
Fax: (510) 658-1834

INTRODUCTION

Dear Bride-to-be,

Congratulations. This is an exciting time in your life! Finally planning that wedding you've always dreamed of. No matter how simple or elaborate – remember, careful and thoughtful planning is the key to a perfect wedding.

Planning a Wedding to Remember was written to help you plan the many details of your wedding, make decisions and keep you organized throughout these busy and emotional pre-wedding months.

Totally revised, my book offers you practical advice, answers to questions, and points of etiquette for today's bride, covering areas of: wording invitations, interfaith marriages, creating your own ceremony, money-saving tips, handling divorced parents, second marriages and much more.

I include various special touches and unique ideas, along with a list of music and flower suggestions which will give you ideas to personalize your wedding and make it even more memorable.

I have provided a number of checklists, guest and gift lists, along with worksheets and handy pockets, to help you budget your time and your money. Also included are monthly planning lists and calendars for both the bride and groom to insure that no detail of your special day will be overlooked. These records will not only keep you organized, but provide you a wonderful momento of your pre-wedding activities for years to come.

May you have the wedding of your dreams...it's all in the planning!

Best wishes,

Beverly Clark

Beverly Clark

WHAT PEOPLE ARE SAYING ABOUT

Planning a Wedding to Remember

"Beverly Clark is recognized as an authority in the area of wedding planning and wedding necessities. Ms. Clark has done a superb job of leading the bride from the time she says, 'I will,' until after she says, 'I do.' This book will help you through the trauma as well as the pleasure of planning a wedding."

Doris Nixon
National Bridal Service

"Everything you ever wanted to know about weddings and special touches too..."

Los Angeles Times

"Beverly Clark has taken the wedding planning process to a new plane...she covers all of the nuts and bolts and teaches you to plan with class and elegance."

Gerard J. Monagham, President
Association of Bridal Consultants

"Planning a Wedding to Remember offers a thorough look at wedding preparations...its suggestions are...practical and useful... will answer just about any wedding question you'll have."

Leonard Maltin on
Video Entertainment Tonight

"An absolute bonanza...author Beverly Clark hasn't left out any detail."

Arthur Stern
Wedding Photographers International

"...one of the most thorough planning tools I've ever seen."
Hallmark Retail Services

"A definite must for anyone planning a wedding."
NBC Network

OTHER BOOKS BY THE AUTHOR

Showers – the complete guide to planning
the perfect bridal and baby shower.

Wedding Memories

Table of Contents

CHAPTER SEVEN
INVITATIONS AND STATIONERY

CHAPTER EIGHT
THE WEDDING PARTY

CHAPTER NINE
BRIDAL GOWN AND ACCESSORIES

CHAPTER TEN
THE WEDDING PARTY ATTIRE

CHAPTER ELEVEN
PLANNING THE RECEPTION

Table of Contents

The Wedding of

_____

&

_____

who were married

on _____

at _____

by _____

CHAPTER ONE

Your Engagement

Congratulations! There's no one more excited than a newly-engaged bride. The next few months will be filled with parties and planning for that special day. The engagement period is also a time of growth and understanding of one another that involves determining mutual goals for a happy life together.

TELLING YOUR FAMILY

Who do you tell first? If your fiancé didn't ask your parents for your hand, which most do not today, then they should be the first to know. If your parents live nearby and know your fiancé, it is best for the two of you to tell them in person. If they do not live nearby, then tell them by phone and try to make arrangements for them to meet your fiancé as soon as possible. I'm sure they will be as excited as you are.

Your fiancé may have already discussed his marriage plans with his parents. In any event, they should be formally told after the fact. It also would be best to tell them in person, but if distance is a problem, a phone call will do. Traditionally, your fiancé's mother will write you a welcoming note or letter; she may do the same for your parents. If she does not write you, don't hesitate to make the first move. It's helpful to get off to a good start by making her feel she is gaining a daughter-in-law rather than losing a son.

TELLING FRIENDS AND RELATIVES

Of course you will now want to phone or write all your close friends and relatives and let them in on the exciting news. Or, you may decide to surprise them all at once, and announce the wonderful news at a family gathering or party. An engagement party may be hosted by you and your fiancé or by your parents.

ENGAGEMENT PARTIES

An engagement party has traditionally been hosted by the bride's parents. However, the party may be hosted by you and your fiancé. Other engagement parties are sometimes hosted by the groom's parents, relatives, or close friends. It's a perfect opportunity to introduce the two families and friends of the couple.

The engagement announcement is generally made during a toast given by the bride's father or her fiancé. A toast is the perfect way to officially fill the guests in on the exciting news, especially when the news may be a surprise to them. The groom's father or other friends may want to join in on the fun and toast the happy couple.

Engagement Party Tips:

• It is a must that you both attend all engagement parties.

• Gifts are generally not given, and should not be expected.

• If a guest chooses to honor the occasion with a gift, accept it graciously and send a thank-you note.

• The party may be a luncheon, brunch, dinner or cocktail party. Any type party would be appropriate.

• Avoid hurt feelings by inviting only those guests that you will also be inviting to your wedding.

• Invitations may be extended by phone or by written invitation, depending on time and formality of the party.

• If formal invitations are sent, and it's not to be a surprise for the guests, then the invitation could read "in honor of Susan Petty and Robert Townsend" or "Please join us in celebrating the engagement of . . . ".

• If the engagement announcement is to be a surprise for the guests, then the invitations should be a general party invitation, not mentioning the couple's names.

• Thank the hosts of your engagement party with a note and a small gift, flowers, or a dinner invitation.

NEWSPAPER ANNOUNCEMENTS

After everyone close to you knows, the time for telling the rest of the world has come.

All proud parents love to see their daughter's picture in the paper. The formal announcement may be placed in both your and your fiancé's local newspapers. Contact the society editor of each paper to find out procedures. Forms are usually available from most local newspapers. Make sure to ask about the picture since many papers only accept a black-and-white photo of the prospective bride. Also, specify the date on which you want the announcement to appear, and provide your name, address, and "please return" on the back of the picture, as well as a stamped envelope to have the picture returned. Obviously, it is not a good idea to include your home address in the article. You will be receiving many lovely gifts over the next several months and there's no need to tip off a burglar about them.

If the parents of the bride are divorced, either parent may announce the engagement, but typically, it is made by the parent with whom the bride has lived. However, both parents should be mentioned in the article. If one parent is deceased, the announcement is made by the surviving parent. If both parents are deceased, the engagement may be announced by a relative, a friend or by the bride herself. The announcement would read "Susan Elizabeth Petty will be married in September to Robert Lee Townsend." Even when the article appears in the groom's parents' local newspaper, they should not be the ones to make the announcement. The word "late" should precede any reference made to a deceased parent.

The engagement should not be announced prior to one year before the wedding and not later than six weeks ahead of the date.

ENGAGEMENT ANNOUNCEMENT EXAMPLE

To appear: _____
(Date)

_____
(Your parents' names)

_____
(Street address)

_____
(City, state, zip code)

_____
(Area code, telephone number)

Mr. and Mrs. _____ of _____ announce the engagement
(your parents' names)   *(their city, if out of town)*

of their daughter, _____, to _____,
(your first and middle names)   *(your fiancé's first and last names)*

the son of Mr. and Mrs. _____ of _____.
(your fiancé's parents' names)   *(fiancé's parents' city)*

No date has been set for the wedding. (Or, The wedding will take place in _____.)
(wedding month)

ENGAGEMENT AND WEDDING RINGS

*S*ince ancient Roman times a plain gold ring has symbolized true and everlasting love. Today, the gold band may be embellished but the symbolism still remains.

SELECTING THE STYLE

If your fiancé hasn't surprised you with the presentation of a ring he selected or a family heirloom that has been handed down through generations, then go shopping and decide together. Although this can be somewhat awkward or touchy, hopefully you have similar taste and budget ideas.

Although some brides (more often second time around) prefer other gems to diamonds, a diamond is the overwhelming choice of today's bride. While the element of surprise is very romantic, the engagement ring is meant to be worn a lifetime, so it's particularly important that the bride-to-be really loves it. Make searching for the perfect ring, one that reflects your personal taste and style, a romantic task, shared by the two of you.

Don't buy in a hurry. The greater your awareness of the elements that determine a diamond or other gem's quality, the better chance you have of getting the best quality ring for your money. Try on several styles to see what fits your taste. If you don't find the ring of your dreams or you want something no one else has, check with your jeweler about making a custom design. Many jewelers offer an opportunity to trade up at a later date, like an anniversary, or you can add diamonds to an existing ring.

It is not necessary to have a diamond engagement ring to signify an official engagement. Many couples prefer to save the money and combine the engagement and wedding ring in one. This can be done nicely with a wider band that is set with a solitaire or inset with many small diamonds. Instead of a smaller diamond, some couples are opting for a larger colored stone such as a ruby, amethyst, sapphire, or emerald. Such colored stones are very popular for second marriages.

Make sure you are dealing with a reliable, reputable jeweler whose advice and assistance will help you make a good selection within your budget. Prices vary tremendously, depending on the type of metal used and the quality of the stone.

Gold is most commonly used for engagement and wedding rings. It is available in either white or yellow and generally 14k or 18k gold is used for these rings. Platinum, which is the strongest and most expensive ring metal, is often used for the prongs which hold the stones.

DIAMONDS

There are four classic criteria when selecting a diamond. The first three – color, cut, and clarity – determine the price per carat. Once that is established, carat weight determines the final price.

Color – The clearer the diamond, the greater its value. Diamonds are graded on a scale. The greater degree of color in the stone, the lower the stone's value, with the exception of very rare colored diamonds which are extremely valuable. Clear or colorless stones are referred to as perfect.

Cut – Accuracy in cutting is essential to the beauty and sparkle of the diamond. The stones are proportioned and faceted to maximize the brilliance through their crowns. The brilliant or round cut is the most common. Other shapes include oval, pear, marquise, emerald cut and heart-shaped.

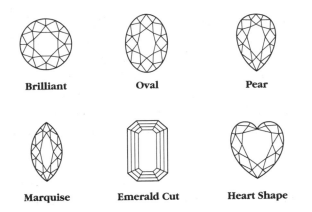

Brilliant	**Oval**	**Pear**
Marquise	**Emerald Cut**	**Heart Shape**

Clarity – This is the term used to describe the degree of inclusions when the stone is magnified ten times. Inclusions are interior or exterior flaws. If they are large and noticeable without a magnifying glass, they will affect the beauty of the stone; otherwise, they will only affect the value. Flawless or perfect stones are stones with no imperfections, and obviously the most valuable and expensive.

Carats: This is the size of the diamond. Color, cut and clarity determine the per carat value. A higher-quality, smaller diamond may be worth more than a lower-quality, larger stone. As the size increases from one carat to over two or three, the price per carat increases tremendously when the stone is of equal quality.

GEMOLOGICAL INSTITUTE OF AMERICA

Fortunately, most jewelers in America either use or recognize the classifications of the Gemological Institute of America. Ask your jeweler for the GIA's rating of color and clarity on each stone you're considering.

The GIA assigns letters of the alphabet to colors, beginning with the letter D as the clearest color and down to the letter L classification (except AD, which is reserved for the very finest jewels).

The GIA also grades the inclusions or imperfections of a stone, which is also important to know in order to comparison shop effectively. Their grading system begins with FL, for flawless diamond, a stone which contains no imperfections that can be seen with a 10x jeweler's loupe. It goes down from there to VVS (very, very small spots), VS (very small spots), all the way to an I_3 diamond, which has obvious imperfections. The average person usually can't find any flaws with the naked eye, down to a VS_2 designation.

Ask your jeweler to show you similar size stones in varying color and clarity, to enable you to select the one that fits both your taste and budget. Once you've determined the size and quality stone you like (for example a .60 carat, K color, VS_1 brilliant cut), then you can compare other similar stones to find the best price.

INSURANCE

The Gemological Institute of America will grade your stone and provide a certificate with unquestionable proof of your diamond's identity as well as its grade. Make sure to get a written guarantee and permanent registration for the diamond when you purchase it. Then get a written appraisal of the replacement value for insurance purposes. Make sure to list the diamond separately on your personal property insurance policy. In the event that you don't have such a policy, see about adding the diamond to your parents' policy temporarily. Have your ring re-appraised every few years and increase your insurance policy accordingly.

SHOPPING TIPS

- Make sure you deal with a reliable, reputable jeweler.

- Choose a jeweler who has been in business for a long time. Ask friends and relatives for recommendations.

- Look for a jeweler (or a store with a gemologist on staff) who has a diploma or certificate from the Gemological Institute of America. This indicates the jeweler has had formal training in his or her field.

- Know approximately the budget you have to work with *before* you start shopping.

- Shop and compare several rings from different jewelers.

- Avoid shops that pressure you to buy on the spot.

- Shop with a note pad to record GIA's designation of the various stones.

- Ask to see samples of diamonds in various colors and clarity grades. You can probably find a stone in the middle of the scale and avoid paying for status you – or anyone else – can't discern.

- Once the size and the GIA color and clarity grade have been determined, then you can compare similar stones for the best price.

- Many reputable jewelers have specials or sales at certain times throughout the year, so do your comparison shopping ahead of time, so you have the knowledge to recognize a good deal and can take advantage of it when it presents itself.

- Call the Better Business Bureau in your area to see if any complaints have been filed against the jeweler.

- Get an outside appraisal of the stone. As a condition of sale, have a qualified independent appraiser look at the stone to ensure the quality which is being represented.

- Ask about returns, guarantees and warranties. Find out if the ring can be returned or exchanged within a certain number of days if there is a discrepancy in the grading, or if the style is not acceptable to the bride. Have this written on your receipt or contract, and get it signed and dated.

- Keep your receipt for insurance purposes. It should describe the details of the ring – the stone's weight, color, clarity, size and cost.

- Find out if there is an extra charge for sizing the ring.

- Ask about repair policy, tightening of the stone and cleaning policy. Be sure to find out if the jeweler's insurance covers any damage to your ring while being repaired.

- If a jeweler has misrepresented a stone, contact the Jewelers Vigilance Committee, 1185 Avenue of the Americas, Suite 2020, New York, New York 10036. Their phone number is (212) 869-9505. This group can investigate your complaint and take action against fraudulent firms in the jewelry business.

- You can get a list of reputable jewelers and appraisers in your area, along with a consumer information kit, by writing to the American Gem Society, 5901 West 3rd Street, Los Angeles, CA 90036, (213) 936-4367

- To get a report on a diamond, contact the Gemological Institute of America in Los Angeles (213) 829-2991 or in New York (212) 221-5858. There is generally a waiting list and a substantial fee for the report.

- Purchase a copy of *Engagement and Wedding Rings*. It is a comprehensive book on diamonds and wedding rings and will tell you just about anything you need to know.

BREAKING THE ENGAGEMENT

Of course, ending an engagement is not pleasant; however, we all make mistakes. A broken engagement is easier to live with than an unhappy marriage.

Start by calling or sending a brief note to family and close friends. A telegram may also be sent depending on the time factor. Remember no explanation is necessary.

Notify your caterer, florist, photographer and officiator as soon as possible. Once this is done, inform the newspapers that carried your formal announcement by sending them a notice similar to this:

Mr. and Mrs. Richard Frye announce the engagement of their daughter, Laura, has ended by mutual consent.

If the invitations have already been sent and time permits, send the guests a printed announcement as follows:

Mr. and Mrs. Richard Frye announce the marriage of their daughter, Laura, to Mr. Charles Wiss will not take place.

Of course, the ring should be given back to your fiancé. Also, any gifts received should be immediately returned to family and friends.

ENGAGEMENT RING WORKSHEET

Stone	#1	#2	#3	#4	#5
Jewelry Store					
Size (number of carats)					
Cut (shape of stone)					
Color (grade D–L)					
Setting (14K, 18K, yellow gold white gold, platinum)					
Price per carat					
Total Price					

Final Choice _____

Stone description _____ price _____

Setting description _____ price _____

Total price _____

Jewelry Store _____

Address _____

Phone No. _____

Sales representative's name _____

Other _____

JEWELRY SHOPPING WORKSHEET

ESTIMATE #1

Store _____ Phone _____ Salesperson _____

Description	Cost
Engagement Ring	_____	_____
Bride's Wedding Ring	_____	_____
Other Jewelry	_____	_____
Total Cost	_____	_____

ESTIMATE #2

Store _____ Phone _____ Salesperson _____

Description	Cost
Engagement Ring	_____	_____
Bride's Wedding Ring	_____	_____
Other Jewelry	_____	_____
Total Cost	_____	_____

JEWELER CHOICE

Name _____   Total Cost _____

Address _____   Deposit Paid _____

Phone _____   Balance Due _____

Salesperson _____   Delivery Date _____

Notes

CHAPTER TWO

The Date and Planning Calendar

With planning, your wedding day will be romantic, exciting and memorable. The first step in planning is to make sure you allow yourself enough time.

The final decision of when to get married is yours and your fiancé's. However, couples often do consult with family members. When the final date has been decided, make sure to let family and close friends know so they can mark it on their calendar to avoid any conflict.

SETTING THE DATE

Some determining factors that influence the date are the time of year you want to be married, the size and formality of your wedding, the availability of the location you want, and possibly your work schedules. These all play an important part in coming up with that special day, so get out your calendar and give them some thought. Then review the list of things that need to be done for the wedding and make sure there's enough time to do them.

If you have your heart set on a location that is popular, you may have to reserve it anywhere from six months to a year ahead of time. With an increase in formal weddings you will be surprised how many locations, caterers and photographers are reserved months in advance. Remember the time flies by quickly. The less time you allow yourself the more flexible you will have to be about the date.

Even if your wedding is small and less formal you should still allow yourself three months, or two at the very least. This would be in the event of a home wedding, a less popular month, or maybe even a weekday wedding. In any case, the wedding gown would have to be made, borrowed, or purchased off the rack (generally dresses must be ordered four to six months before the wedding).

You have the rest of your life to be married, so take your time and enjoy the pre-wedding parties, the shopping, the planning and the excitement before that special day. Then they will become memories that always give you pleasure.

Remember:

• Determine the time of year for your wedding— your favorite season, a special date that's meaningful to you or your groom, etc.

• Consult important family members to avoid conflicts.

• Determine the best time that you can both take time off from work or school.

• Consider your honeymoon plans. Is it a good time of year to honeymoon where you've always dreamed of going?

• Be realistic and allow yourself enough time to plan the wedding you've always wanted.

PLANNING CALENDAR CHECKLIST

The following checklist and calendar are provided so you and the groom can organize your time and planning to insure that you take care of all aspects of your wedding. These are general recommendations and should be adapted to your particular needs.

BRIDE'S CHECKLIST

Six to Twelve Months Before

❏ Select a wedding date and time.
❏ Make a preliminary budget.
❏ Determine your wedding theme or style.
❏ Reserve your ceremony and reception location.
❏ Determine who will officiate at the ceremony.
❏ Hire a wedding consultant, if you plan to use one.
❏ Decide on your color scheme.
❏ Determine the size of the guest list.
❏ Start compiling names and addresses of guests.
❏ Select bridal attendants.
❏ Have fiancé select his attendants.
❏ Plan reception.
❏ Check catering facilities, if at a club or hotel.
❏ Select a caterer, if one is necessary.
❏ Select a professional photographer and videographer.
❏ Select a professional florist.
❏ Select your dress and headpiece.
❏ Announce your engagement in the newspaper.
❏ Select bridesmaids' dresses.
❏ Select engagement ring with fiancé, if he has not already done so.

Four Months Before

❑ Make final arrangement for ceremony (deposits should be paid, contracts signed).

❑ Make sure all bridal attire is ordered.

❑ Have both mothers coordinate and select their dresses.

❑ Register at a bridal registry in the towns of both families.

❑ Order invitations and personal stationery.

❑ Complete the guest lists and compile them in order.

❑ Select the men's wedding attire and reserve the right sizes.

❑ Check requirements for blood test and marriage license in your state.

❑ Make appointment for physical exam.

❑ Shop for wedding rings.

❑ Start planning the honeymoon.

❑ Decide where you will live after the wedding.

❑ Begin shopping for trousseau.

Two Months Before

❑ Address invitations and announcements. They should be mailed 4 to 6 weeks before wedding.

❑ Finalize all details with caterer, photographer, florist, reception hall manager, musicians, etc.

❑ Order wedding cake, if not supplied by caterer.

❑ Finalize ceremony details with officiant.

❑ Make rehearsal arrangements.

❑ Plan rehearsal dinner.

❑ Plan bridesmaids' luncheon.

❑ Make appointments with hairdresser.

❑ Arrange accommodations for out-of-town attendants or guests.

❑ Finalize honeymoon plans.

One Month Before

❑ Have a final fitting for your and bridal attendants' gowns.

❑ Have a formal bridal portrait done.

❑ Complete all physical or dental appointments.

❑ Get blood test and marriage license.

❑ Make transportation arrangements for wedding day.

❑ Purchase gifts for attendants.

❑ Purchase gift for fiancé, if gifts are being exchanged.

❑ Have the bridesmaids' luncheon.

❑ Purchase going away outfit.

❑ Keep a careful record of all gifts received (write thank-you notes immediately instead of letting them pile up).

❑ Make sure you have all accessories, toasting goblets, ring pillow, garter, candles, etc.

❑ Select responsible person to handle guest book and determine its location.

Two Weeks Before

❑ Attend to business and legal details. Get necessary forms to change names on Social Security card, driver's license, insurance and medical plans, bank accounts; make a will.

❑ Prepare wedding announcements to be sent to newspaper.

❑ Reconfirm the accommodations for out-of-town guests.

❑ Arrange to have possessions and gifts moved to your new home. Give a change-of-address card to the post office.

❑ Finish addressing announcements to be mailed on the wedding day.

One Week Before

❑ Contact guests who have not responded.

❑ Give the final count to caterer and review details.

❑ Go over final details with all professional services you have engaged. Inform them of any changes.

❑ Give photographer the list of pictures you want.

❑ Give the videographer a list of shots you would like included in the video.

❏ Give all musicians the lists of music for the ceremony and reception.

❏ Plan the seating arrangements.

❏ Arrange for someone to assist with last-minute errands and to help you dress.

❏ Practice having your hair done to make sure it comes out properly, and determine the time it will take.

❏ Practice using your make-up in the same type of lighting you will have on the wedding date.

❏ Keep up with the writing of your thank-you notes.

❏ Pack your suitcase for the honeymoon.

❏ Make sure you have marriage license.

❏ Make sure you have the wedding rings, and they fit.

❏ Make sure all wedding attire is picked up and fits.

❏ Have a rehearsal with all participants, reviewing their duties.

❏ Attend rehearsal dinner party. Stay calm and enjoy yourself.

❏ Stay with the family the night before the wedding. Get to bed early. You will want to look and feel great the next day.

On the Wedding Day

❏ Be sure to eat something. You have a big day ahead, and many brides have been known to faint.

❏ Take a nice relaxing bath.

❏ Fix hair or have an appointment to have it done at least 3 to 4 hours before the ceremony.

❏ Make sure nails are done. Allow plenty of time to apply make-up. Have all accessories together.

❏ Start dressing one to one-and-a-half hours before the ceremony. If pictures are being taken before the ceremony, then have yourself and attendants ready about two hours before the ceremony (photographer and bridal attendants should arrive forty-five minutes to an hour before the ceremony for pictures).

❏ Have the music start thirty minutes before ceremony.

❏ Have guests seated. Five minutes before the ceremony, have groom's parents seated. Immediately before processional the bride's mother is seated and the aisle runner is rolled out...

After the Wedding

❏ Send announcement and wedding picture to newspapers.

❏ Mail announcements.

❏ Write and mail thank-you notes.

GROOM'S CHECKLIST

Six to Twelve Months Before

❏ Purchase the bride's engagement ring.

❏ Discuss with fiancée the date and type of wedding.

❏ Start on your guest list.

❏ Choose best man and ushers.

❏ Start planning and making necessary arrangements for the honeymoon.

❏ Discuss and plan with fiancée your new home together. If fiancée is moving in with you, start cleaning out closets, cupboards, and drawers to make room for your bride and wedding gifts.

Four Months Before

❏ Shop with fiancée for wedding rings.

❏ Complete your guest list, including full names, addresses and zip codes with phone numbers.

❏ Check requirements for blood test and marriage license in your state, or the state you are being married in.

❏ Select and order men's wedding attire with your fiancée.

❏ Finalize all honeymoon plans and send in deposits if required (don't delay—some resorts fill up fast in popular months).

The Date and Planning Calendar

Two Months Before

❑ Meet with officiant to finalize ceremony details.

❑ Assist parents with plans for the rehearsal dinner party.

❑ Discuss the amount and the financial arrangement for the flowers which are the groom's responsibility.

❑ Arrange accommodations for out-of-town attendants.

One Month Before

❑ See that all attendants have been fitted and wedding attire has been ordered.

❑ Purchase gifts for best man and ushers.

❑ Purchase wedding gift for fiancée, if gifts are being exchanged.

❑ Pick up wedding rings. Make sure they fit.

❑ Take care of business and legal affairs (add bride's name to insurance policies and medical plans, make a new will, add her name to joint checking account or joint charge cards). If you have both agreed to a pre-nuptial agreement, have it drawn up and signed.

Two Weeks Before

❑ Together with fiancée, gather necessary documents and get your marriage license.

❑ Arrange wedding day transportation.

❑ Reconfirm accommodations for out-of-town guests.

❑ If moving, give change-of-address card to post office; arrange to have utilities and phone service turned on in the new home. If not moving, finish cleaning and reorganizing your home; help your fiancée move her things.

❑ Have your hair cut.

The Week Before

❑ Discuss all final details with fiancée; offer to assist if needed.

❑ Pick up and try on wedding attire.

❑ See that attendants get their wedding attire.

❑ Pack clothes for honeymoon.

❑ Reconfirm all honeymoon reservations.

❑ If flying, make sure you have plane tickets.

❑ See to it that you and your attendants are at the rehearsal and that they know their duties.

❑ Go over special seating or pew cards with ushers.

❑ Arrange for gifts brought to the reception to be taken to your new home.

❑ Make sure luggage is in the car or the hotel where you will stay your first night.

❑ Attend rehearsal dinner. Relax and enjoy yourself.

❑ Get to bed early. You want to look and feel your best!

THE WEDDING DAY

❑ Be sure to eat something in the morning.

❑ Allow plenty of time to get dressed (start one hour before ceremony).

❑ Get to the ceremony location on time!

❑ Give the best man the bride's wedding ring.

❑ Place the officiant's fee in a sealed envelope. Give it to the best man so he may present it after the ceremony. Don't forget to take the marriage license to the ceremony, or make sure the best man will bring it.

❑ Have the best man and maid of honor sign the wedding certificate as witnesses.

❑ Dance first with your bride, then with both mothers and the bridesmaids.

❑ Just before leaving the reception, thank the bride's parents, and say good bye to your parents.

Congratulations! You made it—alone at last.

AFTER THE WEDDING

❑ Make sure on the first day of the honeymoon to send flowers or a telegram expressing your appreciation and thanking the bride's parents again for a beautiful wedding and reception.

❑ Take good care of your new bride.

The Date and Planning Calendar

This Month: _____   Months to go: ☐

Sunday	Monday	Tuesday	Wednesday	Thursday	Friday	Saturday

Notes _____

_____

_____

_____

The Date and Planning Calendar

This Month: _____

Months to go: [ ]

Sunday	Monday	Tuesday	Wednesday	Thursday	Friday	Saturday

Notes _____

_____

_____

_____

The Date and Planning Calendar

This Month: _____   Months to go: ☐

Sunday	Monday	Tuesday	Wednesday	Thursday	Friday	Saturday

Notes _____

_____

_____

_____

28

The Date and Planning Calendar

This Month: _____   Months to go: ☐

Sunday	Monday	Tuesday	Wednesday	Thursday	Friday	Saturday

Notes _____

_____

_____

_____

The Date and Planning Calendar

This Month: _____

Months to go: ☐

Sunday	Monday	Tuesday	Wednesday	Thursday	Friday	Saturday

Notes _____

_____

_____

_____

The Date and Planning Calendar

This Month: _____ Months to go: ☐

Sunday	Monday	Tuesday	Wednesday	Thursday	Friday	Saturday

Notcs _____

_____

_____

_____

The Date and Planning Calendar

This Month: _____

Months to go: ☐

Sunday	Monday	Tuesday	Wednesday	Thursday	Friday	Saturday

Notes _____

_____

_____

_____

The Date and Planning Calendar

This Month: _____

Months to go: [ ]

Sunday	Monday	Tuesday	Wednesday	Thursday	Friday	Saturday

Notes _____

_____

_____

_____

The Date and Planning Calendar

This Month: _____   Months to go: ☐

Sunday	Monday	Tuesday	Wednesday	Thursday	Friday	Saturday

Notes
_____
_____
_____
_____

BRIDAL CONSULTANTS

After reviewing the myriad details involved in planning your wedding, you may decide you could use some help. Many women today are busy with careers. They find they don't have time to plan a wedding, or a mother nearby to help with those plans, and find comfort in the advice of an expert. Brides have found hiring an experienced consultant especially helpful when planning a wedding out of town. If you fall into any of these categories, or just would feel more comfortable with a professional on the scene, you may want to consider hiring a bridal consultant. They can help you maximize time and money by making use of their abundant resources and recommending quality services.

Many details involved in the happy, but often hectic, planning process can be handled by a professional consultant. Some consultants offer full-service planning from booking locations to hiring caterers, florists, musicians and supervising the actual wedding on site. Others may be limited to specific areas. Or you may decide you only need someone to supervise the day. So determine what you want to have done, then choose a bridal consultant whose services fit your specific needs. Bridal consultants are there to provide the wedding you dream of; they handle the details, leaving you the time to enjoy your engagement, your family and your fiancé.

DETERMINE THE COST

Though prices often vary according to region and services rendered, the fee you pay may very well be offset by the money and legwork a consultant can save you in the long run. The actual amount you'll pay will depend on your consultant's method of billing. Some charge a flat fee for their services. Others charge a percentage of the total wedding bill, which is usually between 10 and 20 percent. Or your consultant may charge an hourly rate, especially if hired for only limited services. Many use a combination of these methods, depending on the bride's needs. Some may also receive payment from vendors, rather than from the bride.

FINDING A CONSULTANT

To find a good bridal consultant ask other wedding professionals, such as caterers, reception site coordinators, florists, or brides whose weddings you have attended. Or, for a list of bridal consultants, you can write to the Association of Bridal Consultants, 200 Chestnutland Road, New Milford, Connecticut, 06776-2521. Send a legal size, self-addressed and stamped envelope, including your wedding date and phone number. Or call them at (203) 355-0464.

- Interview more than one consultant.

- Find a consultant you feel comfortable working closely with, and one who understands your desires.

- Ask about the number of weddings the consultant has worked on.

- Request client references if you feel you need further reassurance about the consultant's abilities. You must feel confident she can do the job.

- Learn which specific services the consultant offers. Some may handle every detail; others may not.

- Establish the fee structure up front. Is it a flat fee, an hourly rate or a percentage of the wedding costs?

BRIDAL CONSULTANT WORKSHEET

ESTIMATE #1

Name _____ Phone _____

Address _____ Zip _____

Recommended by _____

Appointment Date _____

Services Provided _____

_____

_____

_____

Fee is based on:

❑ Hourly Rate   ❑ Flat fee   ❑ Percentage   ❑ Per Guest

Number of hours of service_____

Consultant choice: Total cost _____

❑ Yes   ❑ No   Deposit $ _____

Contract Signed _____   Balance due $ _____

ESTIMATE #2

Name _____ Phone _____

Address _____ Zip _____

Recommended by _____

Appointment Date _____

Services Provided _____

_____

_____

_____

Fee is based on:

❑ Hourly Rate   ❑ Flat fee   ❑ Percentage   ❑ Per Guest

Number of hours of service_____

Consultant choice: Total cost _____

❑ Yes   ❑ No   Deposit $ _____

Contract Signed _____   Balance due $ _____

CONSULTANT'S INFORMATION WORKSHEET

Wedding Date _____ Time _____

Number of Guests _____

Rehearsal Date _____ Time _____

Name	Home Phone	Work Phone
Bride:		
Groom:		
Bride's Parents:		
Groom's Parents:		

Bride's Attendants	Home Phone	Work Phone
Maid/Matron of Honor:		
Bridesmaid:		
Bridesmaid:		
Bridesmaid:		
Bridesmaid:		
Bridesmaid:		
Junior Bridesmaid:		
Junior Bridesmaid:		
Flower Girl:		
Other:		

Groom's Attendants	Home Phone	Work Phone
Best Man:		
Usher:		
Usher:		
Usher:		
Usher:		
Usher:		
Usher:		
Usher:		
Ringbearer:		
Other:		

CONSULTANT'S INFORMATION WORKSHEET

Ceremony Site _____ Phone _____

Address _____

Area to Dress:

	Yes	No	
	☐	☐	Bride and Attendants
	☐	☐	Groom and Attendants

Reception Site: _____ Phone _____

Address: _____

Area for Bride and Groom to Change: Yes ☐ No ☐

Ceremony Services	Arrival Time	Phone
Officiant:		
Officiant:		
Site Coordinator:		
Organist:		
Soloist:		
Other Musician:		
Photographer:		
Videographer:		
Florist:		
Wedding Transportation:		
Other		

Reception Services	Arrival Time	Phone
Site Coordinator:		
Guest Book Attendant:		
Gift Attendant:		
Florist:		
Caterer:		
Bakery:		
Bartender:		
Rent Equipment:		
Special Transportation:		
Musicians:		
Other:		
Other:		

CHAPTER THREE

Your Wedding Style

*Y*our wedding style should reflect your desires and those of your fiancé, and may also be determined by the number of guests or the size of your budget. Today there are many alternatives and various combinations of wedding styles that are acceptable. No matter how formal the wedding, it is best to keep style and color similar throughout. They make up a theme you should try to maintain from the invitation to the time you leave the reception.

Whichever style you choose, the main point is to carry it out well. Remember, a well-planned and smoothly organized wedding makes a perfect wedding.

DECIDING ON FORMALITY

Formal and semi-formal weddings take place in the daytime or in the evening. The number of guests invited, time of the ceremony, and the bride's attire determine the degree of formality for the entire wedding party. The following are some basic guidelines as to what is standard with each degree of formality.

Very Formal

Usually held in a church, synagogue, temple or hotel. Includes engraved invitations, formal photography, a large and elaborate sit-down dinner or buffet. Generally includes an orchestra for dancing and floral displays for the tables. May involve the help of a bridal consultant.

The bridal party consists of between four and twelve attendants: a maid or matron of honor, the best man, bridesmaids, one usher for every 50 guests, one or two flower girls and a ringbearer.

Formal

Formal weddings are very popular. Besides being held in a place of worship, they may be held in a home or garden. They include the traditional elements of a bridal gown, attendants, formal invitations, music, floral displays and usually a meal.

Semi-formal

Location choices for both ceremony and reception may vary and often both are held at the same place. Engraved invitations do not have to include separate response cards. However, you will have more R.S.V.P.'s if they are included. Semi-formal weddings usually have fewer attendants, and the choice of wedding attire and flowers are less traditional and more individual.

Informal

There is a wide range and variety of informal weddings. They can all be made just as special as the most expensive formal wedding, as long as they are kept in good taste. Many informal weddings are second marriages, and often take place in the daytime. Appropriate wedding attire might be a street or ankle length dress, or a suit in white or pastel. The invitations may be as informal as a hand written note. The site for the ceremony may be a private home or garden, with flowers and decorations being optional. The refreshments may consist of champagne, punch and cake, or cocktails and hors d'oeuvres.

SELECTING THE CEREMONY LOCATION

The location of your ceremony may be selected for a number of reasons. Among them are religious reasons and individual taste.

Perhaps there is a location at which you have always dreamed of being married. In any case, when looking for a site for the ceremony and reception, make sure the space will accommodate all your guests. On the other hand, don't select a large church or temple if there are very few guests. A small place of worship would be more intimate.

CHURCH OR SYNAGOGUE

When planning a religious wedding, the selection will depend on either your, your finance's or your family's personal affiliation with a particular church or synagogue. Keep in mind the location's distance from the reception, and its size and style in relation to your overall wedding plans.

Questions to Ask

Before making a commitment to a particular place of worship, set up an appointment to discuss the following:

• Is proof of divorce or special permission from the church needed when remarrying?

• Must we be members of the church, or may a friend sponsor us?

- Is premarital counseling required? If so, for how long?

- What are the fees for the church or synagogue? And how much time does that allow us?

- Is a small chapel available for smaller ceremonies?

- Are there any restrictions regarding ceremony attire, such as bare shoulders or yarmulkes?

- How many people will the church or synagogue hold?

- Are the facilities available for a reception; if so, is there an additional fee?

- May rice, bird seed or rose petals be thrown?

- Are there accommodations for wheelchairs?

- Is an aisle runner, chuppah, candelabra or kneeling cushion available if needed?

- May the wording of the religious ceremony be changed at all?

- Are there facilities for the bridal party to dress?

- Are there any restrictions regarding flowers or candles?

- What are the rules regarding photography inside the place of worship?

- Are there music restrictions that interfere with music or songs you may want?

- Do you need approval for special vows you may want to incorporate?

- Are there restrictions regarding the day of the week, or the time the ceremony can take place? What about religious holidays?

- What are the policies on interfaith marriages? Can you combine two religious ceremonies, or have both clergymen officiate jointly?

PRIVATE CLUBS OR HOTEL

These settings are popular if your emphasis is not on a very formal or extremely religious ceremony. One advantage is that most of these locations can accommodate both the ceremony and reception. Many will even furnish altars, aisle, canvas, canopies and chairs. Before committing yourself, make sure you check on these items and if they are not provided, see what the availability and cost will be through a rental company.

Hotel facilities are available to everyone, but popular hotels tend to book up rapidly, especially in the traditionally busy wedding months of June, July and August.

Private clubs are nice, but few open their facilities to non-members. If your family does not have a membership, you might have a relative or close friend who would be honored to host (not pay for) your wedding.

HOME OR GARDEN WEDDINGS

Depending on the style of wedding and the size of your home or garden, there's a special warmth and uniqueness that can be derived from a home wedding.

A home or garden wedding can range from a more formal ceremony and catered affair to an informal ceremony and a do-it-yourself reception (with a little help from your friends). If your home isn't large enough, maybe some friends or relatives would offer the use of theirs.

If the ceremony is in the home, a nice entrance can be made by coming down a stairway, and then having the ceremony take place in front of a fireplace. If in the garden, what about having the ceremony under a stately old tree or a decorated arch or gazebo? Whatever the focal point is, try to position it so the sun will not shine in the guests' eyes. Depending on space, guests may be seated or may stand. If the latter is the case, don't make the ceremony too long. Also, when you're planning a ceremony outside, make sure the area can be tented or the ceremony moved inside in the event of bad weather.

If your home is not large enough, and you don't want to borrow a friend's or relative's, sometimes you can find private homes to rent through real-estate companies, wedding consultants or local newspapers. It may be possible to go through a company that finds locations for advertisements or television commercials. So check to see if your city has this kind of company.

SHIPS OR BOATS

These are great for smaller, more unconventional weddings, which can certainly be fun. If you don't have a ship or boat to borrow, check the yellow pages or local newspapers in your area regarding rentals. Price will vary according to the size of the vessel and the number of hours you rent it. In most cases you will provide the catered food, whether it be an elaborate buffet dinner or simply cake and coffee. Larger ships, such as cruise ships, will provide the food for you.

MOUNTAINS, PARKS, BEACHES

For some there is nothing more romantic than saying your vows under a beautiful blue sky. The Parks and Recreation Department in your area can help you find that perfect spot. Parks, mountains or beaches are wonderful locations for theme weddings. You could have a Hawaiian wedding at the beach, followed by the traditional luau for the reception. Or have the wedding in a beautiful park with an old fashioned picnic reception. This can be made interesting and fun by giving each couple their own picnic basket filled with a variety of food, a bottle of wine and a decorative table cloth.

WINERIES

If you have wineries in your area, many of them will rent their grounds. The prices can vary so it may be wise to check a few before making a decision. Many are old, steeped in tradition, and make a beautiful setting for a unique wedding. Some wineries in California's Napa Valley are known for the hot-air balloons which land at the winery in time for a champagne brunch. You can plan an early morning ceremony, then take a hot-air balloon ride to a winery where you will meet your guests for a champagne brunch.

HISTORICAL OR PUBLIC SITES

There are many beautiful old mansions that, over the years, have been donated to cities or states, and are open to the public for tours. Many of these mansions can be rented. The cost varies so check their fees and availability. To imagine using such a location, just think of having a Gatsby style wedding at the Astors' mansion in Newport, Rhode Island, where the movie "The Great Gatsby" was filmed.

There are also many museums, arboretums and formal gardens which make beautiful settings for a wedding. To find locations that are available in your area check local newspapers and phone books, or call the Chamber of Commerce in your area.

CEREMONY LOCATION IDEAS

• Private Clubs

• Elks, Women's Clubs, etc. facilities

• Community centers

• Condominium or private estate clubhouse facilities

• Banks or large lobbies of grand old buildings

• Civic or private theaters

• Art galleries

• Museums

- Historical buildings or mansions
- Private homes or estates
- Public beaches, parks or gardens
- Zoos or amusement parks
- Fairgrounds or racetracks
- Movie studio lots
- Wineries, ranches or orchards
- Bed and Breakfast Inns
- Romantic restaurants
- Hotel ballrooms
- University chapels
- Churches or Synagogues
- Yachts, boats, barges
- A romantic resort
- Military Club facilities
- Your home or that of a friend

CHOOSING THE CEREMONY TIME

Once you have decided on the date and have a good idea of the type and style of your wedding, you're ready to select a time. This may be determined by your own personal choice, religious desires, or the type of reception your budget allows.

Most of the fashionable Catholic weddings are celebrated with a Nuptial High Mass at noon. If you prefer Low Mass, then ten o'clock is a nice hour. And the simplest of Catholic ceremonies, celebrated in the church without Mass, may take place in the afternoon.

Protestant ceremonies seem to favor hours of either four to four-thirty in the afternoon, or an earlier time of twelve to twelve-thirty, if you're planning to serve a lunch. Two o'clock to three-thirty are nice hours for ceremonies that will be followed by a teatime reception.

Evening ceremonies usually begin between the hours of six and eight o'clock.

Whichever hour you select, your wedding can range from the simplest to the most formal. Formality, in this case, refers to the degree of correctness and charm, not the degree of pompousness. Remember the amount of formality in your wedding should be complemented by the same amount in your reception.

UNIQUE CEREMONIES

Here are some unique ceremonies that have been performed. Usually better for smaller or second weddings, these ceremonies are definitely made for the non-traditional and the adventurous.

- A couple that loved to ski said their vows on top of a snow-covered mountain. They found an officiant who also skied, and invited whichever family and friends they wanted to have there.

- A surfer who loved the water, and being in it, decided to gather an officiant and some friends, and paddled just outside the surfbreak. The vows were said as everyone gathered together on their surfboards.

- Another couple had their guests gathered in a park, waiting for the ceremony to begin. The bride, groom and officiant surprised the crowd when they came floating down with parachutes. The vows were said, the landing was safe, the ceremony finished, and the reception began.

- If you would like a little more time in the air, then saying the vows in a hot-air balloon would probably suit you better. Although it may be more difficult to land where you want, it will certainly be a memorable experience.

CEREMONY LOCATION WORKSHEET

	ESTIMATE #1		ESTIMATE #2	
	Name _____		Name _____	
	Phone _____		Phone _____	
	Description	Cost	**Description**	Cost
CEREMONY SITE Date available Time available Occupancy Rental fee				
OFFICIANT Name Phone Fee				
SERVICE Organist Soloist Altar boys Other				
EQUIPMENT Aisle runner Canopy Kneeler Altar Other				
RESTRICTIONS Photography Candles Music Rice/Roses petals Other				
MISCELLANEOUS				
TOTAL				

CEREMONY CHOICE

Name _____

Address _____

Phone _____

Date/Time _____

OFFICIANT CHOICE

Name _____

Address _____

Phone _____

Date/Time _____

WEDDING INFORMATION WORKSHEET

WEDDING DATE _____ Time _____

Style of Wedding   ❑ Formal   ❑ Semiformal   ❑ Informal

Approximate Number of Guests: _____

Number of Attendants   Bride: _____ Groom: _____

Additional Attendants: ❑ Flower Girl   ❑ Ringbearer
                       ❑ Guestbook Attendant   ❑ Gift Attendant

COLOR SCHEME: _____
_____
_____

OFFICIANT: _____ Phone _____

Special Classes or Requirements: _____

Dates: _____ Time _____

Location: _____

CEREMONY SITE: _____ Phone: _____

Address: _____

Restrictions: _____

Special Requirements: _____

Equipment Needed: _____

Decorating Ideas: _____
_____
_____

Rehearsal Date: _____ Time: _____

RECEPTION SITE: _____ Phone: _____

Address: _____

Reception Site Reserved: From _____ Until _____

Restrictions: _____

Special Requirements: _____

Equipment Needed: _____
_____

Decorating Ideas: _____
_____
_____

NEW WAYS TO WED

Brides and grooms today are adding a fresh twist to the old traditions of marriage, twists limited only by their imagination.

How are these new trends different from those of the past?

These are celebrations that express the needs and desires of people marrying in the 1990s. They reflect changing times; couples who are marrying when they are older, or for a second time, couples whose families and friends are scattered around the country.

Brides and grooms today are looking to make a personal statement about who they are by using creative wedding themes, unique locations and imaginative ceremonies. These couples and their families are celebrating like never before with large, lavish and creative celebrations. Above all, they are making them memorable and fun.

WEEKEND WEDDINGS

Probably the most common new trend in weddings is the weekend wedding. This is a wedding where friends and relatives come from around the country to join other guests in a weekend reunion of parties and activities. Having a weekend of events gives everyone a chance to spend time together—and guarantees unforgettable fun.

More and more couples are planning weekend weddings, since many are no longer marrying in the town where family and friends are. This provides an incentive for guests to travel from far away; your wedding becomes a catalyst for a family reunion and a memorable gathering.

It does not have to be as expensive as you might think, and can give others a chance to get involved. The following are some ideas:

Friday – You might start the weekend by having a friend or relative host a welcoming party Friday evening, or expand the rehearsal dinner to include out-of-town guests.

Saturday – A luncheon, picnic or barbecue can be hosted by another relative or friend, followed by an afternoon of activities. Plan a golf tournament, tennis match, or game of croquet. Everyone is invited.

Saturday evening—A formal evening wedding and reception, starting at 6:00 or 6:30 p.m., would make the perfect ending to a great day.

Sunday—The bride and groom stay in town to greet their guests at a late morning garden brunch, followed by an afternoon softball game.

Sunday evening—The bride and groom may choose to say their good-byes and leave for their honeymoon as guests leave at their leisure. Or they may all decide to stay for a Pizza Party that evening and say their good-byes over coffee and muffins the next morning.

The plan above is just to give you an example; the options are endless. The following are some ideas for parties and activities:

• Barbecue and pool party.

• Picnic at the beach or a park.

• Organize a golf or tennis tournament.

• Play a softball game.

• Hire a cartoonist, astrologer or magician to entertain guests at an evening event.

• Host a Hawaiian luau.

Guests will need plenty of time to plan for this fun-filled weekend, so send a preliminary itinerary or announcement well in advance of the actual wedding invitation. As the date approaches, send a schedule of the activities and parties that are planned. Mention any additional costs guests might incur for an activity, and tip them off to the appropriate attire; shorts, jeans, bathing suits, or formal attire. Include information on travel or lodging arrangements. Even though guests are responsible for their own travel and hotel costs, you might try to reserve a group of rooms at a reduced rate. Any savings would be much appreciated.

HONEYMOON WEDDINGS

The Honeymoon Wedding can be similar to a Weekend Wedding; however, it invites guests to travel to a romantic vacation spot. There they enjoy a few days of fun with the bride and groom. Tying the knot in a uniquely romantic location, be it a beautiful beach in Mexico, Hawaii or the Caribbean, or on a ski slope in Aspen or the French Alps, the Honeymoon Wedding is an experience all will remember.

Today many couples are choosing to celebrate their weddings at an ideal honeymoon location – this is especially well-suited for couples who have children from previous marriages. It allows children to feel included and provides time for the two families to spend time together. Other couples opt for this type of wedding because it allows them to keep the celebration small and intimate, whereas having the wedding in their home town may necessitate inviting 300 guests. The Honeymoon Wedding, however, can be as intimate and informal or as large and elaborate as you'd like it to be.

The budget for the Honeymoon Wedding will vary according to the size of the reception and other parties or dinners you choose to host. Typically, the guests, with the exception of younger children or older parents who may not be able to afford the trip on their own, pay for their own airfare and accommodations.

There are a number of variations and combinations, again depending on what you can afford and what you choose to pay for. If a large number of people will be attending, you should check airlines and hotels for group rates. In many cases, the guests stay only a few days, and the bridal couple decides to remain for a longer time, or perhaps to move on to another location for some private time before returning home.

Wedding Ideas

The following are a few Honeymoon Wedding ideas; the options are only limited by your imagination and your budget. Contact your travel agent to get ideas, order a copy of my video "Romantic Honeymoon Destinations," or think of a location that already has a special meaning for you.

- A tropical location – Hawaii, Bermuda, the Caribbean, Mexico, Puerto Rico.

- A cruise ship or river boat.

- A train trip, perhaps the Orient Express.

- If your hobby is bicycling, then a bicycle tour in the Wine Country.

- For those who prefer a rustic getaway, what about a dude ranch, camping at a favorite lake, or renting houseboats?

- If your budget's unlimited, charter a plane and fly your guests to your favorite castle in Scotland, or cruise the Mediterranean on a private yacht.

- Plan a ski Honeymoon Wedding – there are a large number of great resorts, both in the United States and abroad.

- Make it a cultural experience with a trip to Egypt, Israel, Greece or Japan.

- Check local resort towns near your wedding site, to which guests could drive.

- For more ideas, pick up travel magazines, bridal magazines or travel books about an area you're considering.

Before you set your heart on any one particular spot, you'll have to do some investigation of the rules and requirements for marrying there. Every state has different laws and regulations. Some countries make it almost impossible to be married there; France requires a thirty day residency prior to the wedding, and other countries require even longer stays. Bermuda makes it easy by requiring only a "Notice of Intended Marriage" be published in the newspaper three weeks before the marriage, which can be arranged in advance long distance.

Planning Tips:

- If marrying in the United States, call the county clerk's office or marriage license bureau in the city where you plan to be married.

- If you are planning to marry in a foreign country, contact its consulate or tourist board, or write to the American Embassy in that country.

- Allow plenty of time – the marriage application period may be lengthy.

- Be prepared to gather endless documents and certificates. Some that probably will be required would include: proof of citizenship; notarized birth certificate; affidavit stating neither person is currently married; blood test; proof of divorce or death certificate, if it pertains to your situation. If you find the documentation and time requirements too much trouble to deal with, consider having a legal marriage at home im-

mediately before traveling to the foreign country, where a ceremony and reception can then be held.

- Couples who have their hearts set on marrying abroad, but have found requirements by foreign countries to be more than they care to handle, should consider Hawaii, the United States Virgin Islands, Jamaica or Puerto Rico as alternatives. You'll find them much easier to deal with.

- To marry at sea you would need to hold the ceremony while the ship is in port, or within three miles of land. You would need a marriage license from the state or country in whose waters you are to be married. Arrangements must be made with the ship's captain ahead of time.

- Check with your state to see if it recognizes out-of-country marriages.

PROGRESSIVE WEDDING

A Progressive Wedding is a perfect choice for a couple whose families and friends live in different parts of the country, or for a bride or groom with divorced parents who don't want to attend the same event.

This type of wedding is a great alternative when not everyone you'd like to celebrate with can travel to the same location; the bride and groom simply travel to them.

Let's say the bride's family lives in New York, the groom's family is in Los Angeles, and the couple now lives in Texas where many of their friends are. The wedding ceremony and reception hosted by the bride's parents would be in New York. Then the couple would travel to Los Angeles to a reception given by the groom's parents for his family and friends. Upon returning home to Texas they, or a close friend, host a reception for those friends who were unable to attend the other two.

Those receptions following the original ceremony may be as formal as the first wedding reception, informal, or anything in between. Some brides choose to repeat the original ceremony and wear their wedding gown again at a formal reception. Many others choose to wear an ankle length gown or a dressy cocktail dress instead.

The Progressive Wedding can relieve the financial burden of guests who wouldn't want to miss your celebration, but can't really afford travel and accommodation costs. This is becoming a practical alternative for today's brides. It can also be the perfect solution in a situation where the groom's family wants to invite more guests than the bride's family is able to accommodate.

SURPRISE WEDDING

The Surprise Wedding is a new trend growing in popularity, especially among couples who are marrying for the second or third time. This is a perfect celebration for those who don't want family and friends to make a fuss, or feel obligated to send a gift. Usually both the bride and groom are in on the secret. However, if the groom is confident and daring, he may decide to surprise the bride with a proposal and ceremony at the same time. Since most brides prefer to be involved in the planning process of this special day, I recommend surprising her only with the proposal at some prior time, then jointly planning the surprise wedding for family and friends.

The spontaneity of this wedding ceremony turns the event into an emotional and festive occasion for all. The couple may host the party themselves under the pretense of a birthday, house-warming, or no-special-occasion party. Or you may enlist the help of a friend who appears to be just having a party. A Surprise Wedding can be as informal and intimate, or large and elaborate as you'd like it to be.

Surprise Your Guests

The following are some tips and imaginative ideas to surprise your guests and make a memorable day for both of you—and probably an occasion your guests won't forget either!

- The party may be hosted at a home, restaurant, hotel, garden, on a yacht—or just about anywhere.

- Host a Halloween costume party where you and your fiancé come dressed as bride and groom; invite the officiant to dress appropriately.

- Invite your guests to a black tie New Year's Eve party. Say your vows just before the stroke of midnight; then everyone can join in the celebration by kissing the bride and groom.

- Have guests arrive at your home for what they think is a party, offer them a glass of champagne—then load them into waiting limousines, vans, trolleys or horsedrawn carriages that will take them to the church for a surprise ceremony. Afterward, they will be transported to an elaborately decorated reception site to continue celebrating with more champagne and food.

- Invite guests to a barbecue, birthday, housewarming, or no-special-occasion party. Then surprise them with the wedding ceremony. To ensure guests dress appropriately, state the dress on the invitation—casual, formal or black tie.

- Don't forget, even though it's a surprise, you will still need to make prior arrangements with an officiant and obtain your marriage license.

- Plan a trip or vacation with a group of close friends. Then surprise them all by getting married on the trip, turning the event into a Honeymoon Wedding (see that section for further details).

- Plan a family reunion with aunts, uncles, cousins and grandparents. You may want to invite a few close friends to drop by just in time for the surprise ceremony.

Notes

_____
_____
_____
_____
_____
_____
_____
_____
_____
_____
_____
_____
_____
_____
_____
_____
_____
_____
_____
_____
_____
_____
_____

CHAPTER FOUR

Your Wedding Ceremony

Most brides-to-be have always fantasized about their wedding day. How wonderful and beautiful it can be! Determining the type of wedding is a decision that should be made by both you and your fiancé according to your personal preference and religious beliefs. The size and style of the wedding will be determined by your desires, the location and your budget.

If you and your fiancé both have similar religious backgrounds, this decision may be easier. However, it is important and should be discussed so that you both feel comfortable. If you are of different denominations, you may mutually agree on one religious ceremony, try to combine ideas from both, or create your own ceremony. Make sure you are aware of all practices, beliefs, and regulations of the congregation you select.

RELIGIOUS CEREMONIES

Roman Catholic Ceremonies

Marriage, to the Catholic Church, is considered a serious and lasting commitment. Marriage being one of the seven sacraments, most parishes require pre-marital counseling so the couple can prepare for their life together.

If both are Catholic, marriage banns must be announced three times—during Mass on Sundays or holy days, or in the Church calendar of both the bride's and groom's parishes. With an interfaith marriage, banns are not published. The Catholic must obtain dispensation from the bishop of the diocese. In the case of divorced Catholics, a church-sanctioned annulment is required before they may remarry.

The Church discourages weddings from taking place on Sunday or holy days and after 6:00 p.m. on Saturdays. They also require that traditional vows be said, although slight changes may be possible as long as the meaning remains the same. The most traditional and religious ceremony is one that takes place at high noon—a Nuptial Mass. You may also want to include one or both of the following symbolic rituals: the bride places the bouquet at the shrine or statue of Mary while a prayer is said, or you both light one larger unity candle from two smaller ones to signify your new life as one.

In the case of an interfaith marriage, a priest will usually agree to co-officiate with a Protestant minister. The two ceremonies are similar. However, in the traditional Catholic procession, the father escorts the bride down the aisle but does not "give her away." Most interfaith marriages do not have a Nuptial Mass, and in those that do, communion is not taken by the non-Catholics. With an interfaith ceremony, a combination of both religious traditions is best.

Eastern Orthodox

The churches of the Eastern rite, including Russian and Greek Orthodox, are similar in many ways to the Catholic tradition. Interfaith marriages are allowed, providing the non-Orthodox party is a baptized Christian. Remarriages are also acceptable if religious decrees of annulment have been received, followed by a civil divorce. The banns of marriage may be published or not, as desired.

The Orthodox ceremony is long and full of symbolism. It usually takes place in the afternoon or early evening, but not during seasons of fasting or certain holy days. The ceremony begins with a betrothal ritual in which the rings are blessed, exchanged three times to signify the Holy Trinity and then placed on the bride's and groom's right hands.

At the close of the betrothal ritual, two crowns are placed on the heads of the bride and groom and are exchanged three times. A Gospel is read; the couple then drink from the same glass of wine three times. This signifies their everlasting love and commitment to share both the happy and sad times in marriage. The ceremony closes with the bride and groom, hands bound together, being led around a ceremonial table three times while the congregation sings "God Grant Them Many Years."

Jewish Ceremonies

Orthodox, Conservative, and Reform are the three groups within the Jewish religion, with Orthodox being the most strict in following the Jewish law. Conservative falls in the middle, while Reform is the most liberal of the three.

Some of the differences between the traditions are as follows: In the Orthodox interpretation the rabbi will not marry divorced persons unless they have a religious as well as civil decree. The men and women are seated in separate areas of the synagogue. Even though the

Conservative ceremony is less rigid in adhering to the Jewish law, many of the traditions are the same as the Orthodox. With both, the service is in Hebrew and Aramaic. Neither a Conservative nor Orthodox rabbi will officiate at a marriage of mixed faiths. The wedding attire is very conventional. The men wear caps or yarmulkes in these ceremonies. Another similarity is that the ring is placed on the index finger of the bride's right hand during the ceremony (it may be switched to the left hand after the ceremony). The ceremonies are performed under a chupah by a rabbi.

The Reform service is in Hebrew and English. The ceremony is generally performed under a chupah, but this is not mandatory. The chupah is a canopy which symbolizes cohabitation and consummation. Men may wear yarmulkes, if they desire. In some Reform ceremonies the ring may be placed directly on the bride's left hand during the ceremony.

The Jewish wedding may take place at any time, other than on the Sabbath, during Passover, or other holy days.

The ceremony ends with the reciting of the seven blessings. The bride and groom drink the blessed wine from a glass, the glass is wrapped in a napkin, then smashed beneath the groom's foot.

There are different beliefs for the act of smashing the glass. One represents an expression of sadness over the destruction of the Temple in Jerusalem in 70 B.C. This is to remind the bride and groom of their obligation to rebuild Zion, and that even in the midst of the festivities, they must not forget that life is not all happiness. As with many cultures throughout the world, the making of noise is considered a manner in which to ward off evil spirits, which the superstitious believe will want to harm the good fortune of the bride and groom.

Many times "mazel tov" is said at the end of the ceremony. This means good star or good position of your stars, which, over the years, has come to mean good fortune.

Protestant Ceremonies

While most Protestant churches have similar marriage ceremonies, each sect has its own practices and traditions. It is best to go over the regulations of the church with the clergy member that you select. Some are reluctant to perform a marriage on Sundays or holy days, although it is allowed. Then, too, churches may have restrictions against certain music, the use of candles, or photography. And many churches will require both of you to attend pre-marital counseling sessions with a clergyman.

Interfaith marriages are accepted in most sects, as long as one partner is a baptized member of that sect. In the case of divorced persons, a "church judgement" as well as civil divorce papers may be required.

In Protestant ceremonies the bride is escorted down the aisle and given away by her father. If he is not available, a brother, relative or close friend may escort her, or she may choose to walk down the aisle alone.

Most fathers look forward to the moment when they are asked, "Who giveth this woman to be married to this man?" Traditionally, he answers "Her mother and I do," places her hand in the groom's, and then takes his seat in the front left row. The marriage vows end with "til death do us part." And many go on to finish the ceremony with the Lord's Prayer.

OTHER CEREMONIES

Civil Ceremony

A civil ceremony is performed by a judge or authorized official, and may take place in a courthouse, or judge's chambers. Civil ceremonies of this type are ideal for small informal weddings, and often the choice for remarriages or couples with religious differences. A small reception may immediately follow or a larger celebration may be held at a later time.

Popular locations for larger civil ceremonies include: homes, gardens, clubs or hotels. The procedures would follow that of a religious ceremony in dress and formality. A reception of like style and formality usually follows immediately.

Military Ceremony

Traditional military ceremonies usually take place at military chapels. However, other locations are sometimes used. The groom and military attendants dress in appropriate uniforms (white in summer, blue in winter). Officers carry a sword or saber, and boutonnieres are never worn. An arch of sabers, swords or rifles, which the new couple walks through, is formed at the exit of the ceremony and/or the entrance to the reception.

Non-military attendants, fathers, and the bride should dress in traditional formal attire. If the bride is a military officer she may opt to wear her dress uniform.

The Double Ceremony

One double wedding can cut down the expense of holding two separate weddings, especially if the couples include family members, two sisters, or brother and sister, where a great many of the guests would have been the same for both.

There are different ways of conducting the ceremony. The younger bride may follow the older one down the aisle, they may choose to use the same bridal party, or each may have her own. It all depends on the available space and individual situation.

PERSONALIZING YOUR CEREMONY

Today more and more couples are composing their own, or a portion of their own, ceremony. There are a number of ways you and your fiancé can add that personal, creative touch to your wedding. You may want to write your own vows or change some of the words of traditional vows. Whatever you decide, give a typed copy to the officiant a few weeks before the ceremony so he or she can become familiar with it. You both may want the officiant to read the vows or you may choose to read the vows to each other. In this event, be sure to keep a copy for yourselves and go over them until you feel comfortable with the lines. It's wise to keep the bride's and groom's speaking parts short since it's so easy to forget your lines in the excitement and emotion of the moment.

IDEAS FOR A CREATIVE CEREMONY

- Discuss with your officiant which portion, if any, of the traditional wording may be changed.

- Rather than have your back to the guests, change places with the officiant and face your guests.

- At a small, intimate ceremony, have the guests join you at the altar or have them join hands encircling you.

- Include both sets of parents in the processional.

- Have the groom meet you half-way down the aisle.

- The bride can part from her father by kissing him on the cheek when they reach his seat, then walk alone to meet the groom.

- Have the officiant ask "Who blesses this union?" or "Who blesses this marriage?" Have both sets of parents or all the guests join in saying "We do."

- Some brides and grooms are each writing his or her own vows, therefore making the vows different from one another. They may even choose to keep these promises secret until the wedding day.

- Involve children from previous marriages by acknowledging them in the ceremony through special readings, prayers or the presentation of the "Family Medallion." (More about this in the chapter on second marriages.)

- The vows themselves should only take two or three minutes to repeat or recite to one another. Additional thoughts on your commitment to marriage may be expressed in the main body of the ceremony or through the use of special poems and prayers.

- Have a favorite piece of music played, or song sung, as you go down the aisle, something other than the traditional wedding march. Music meaningful to the two of you could also be sung or played during the ceremony or as you leave. But check with your church or synagogue as to any music restrictions they might have.

- Write your own poem or prayer and read it, or have quotations from a favorite poem or prayer read by the officiant or a family member.

- You may want to print a program to be given to all the guests as they enter. It could include the names of your attendants and who they are or how you met them, a special poem or prayer or your wedding vows. Such a program gives a nice personal touch, especially to a large ceremony, and serves as a remembrance to take home.

- Depending on your budget and the number of people, a single rose could be handed to every guest, or a candle for the guest to light during an evening ceremony.

- If you are not too nervous, you can stop at the end of the aisle, take a single rose from your bouquet and hand it to your mother. Then take another and hand it to his mother. Keep this move as a little surprise for them.

- Incorporate symbolism in some way by carrying a family Bible, handkerchief or fan that was carried by your or the groom's mother.

- In a church wedding, you can find out about having the church bells rung after you say your vows.

- There are creative alternatives to throwing rice. Since rice can cause harm to the birds who may eat it, consider having birdseed thrown instead of the traditional rice. Dried rose petals, colorful confetti or streamers (in bio-degradable material) are affordable alternatives. Or add some fun by having guests blow bubbles as the newlyweds leave the church. Sparklers (when carefully used and discarded) can be spectacular for an evening wedding.

- Add a romantic touch to your nuptials, with the centuries-old European tradition of releasing white doves, the symbol of love, unity and devotion, after being pronounced husband and wife. With the church ceremony, stage the dove release outside. Re-exit the church, and have the doves released as your guests look on. A flock of white doves makes a great alternative to throwing rice, and a spectacular send-off. For information on white dove releases, check the wedding section of your phone book's yellow pages or call local florists and pet stores. This special touch may not be available in your area.

- Today's ecology-minded brides who are looking for new ways to do something special for their weddings and the environment, might consider the newest concept in weddings, and release dozens of Monarch butterflies. These butterflies are specifically raised for this purpose, then carefully shipped overnight, to be released into the environment at the proper time during the ceremony. This not only helps increase our diminishing butterfly population; but adds a dazzling touch to a garden wedding. For information regarding butterfly releases, contact Swallowtail Farms at (916) 966-7952.

Acceptance Ceremony

If you're a bride who is looking for an alternative to being "given away," the "Acceptance Ceremony " may be the perfect substitute for this portion of the wedding ceremony. Many brides who are older, or who are marrying for a second time, feel being "given away" isn't appropriate in their situations. Other brides who do not have a father in attendance find this a nice alternative to selecting an honorary person to give them away.

In the "Acceptance Ceremony," the officiant asks if there are family members from both the bride's and groom's families who wish to stand and express a few words accepting the new spouse into their family. The officiant may start with either the bride's or groom's family first. Ahead of time, select one or two relatives from each side to speak, so they will have something prepared. Others may choose to join in after the originally-chosen members have spoken. If either the bride or groom has children from a previous marriage, those children should be included in the ceremony and should be accepted into the

new family along with the parent. Be sure they are mentioned by name in the speech.

Candlelight Ceremonies

A candlelight ceremony can be beautiful in the evening, or in the late afternoon with the lights dimmed. One way is to have two candle stands decorated with ribbons and flowers, placing one on either side of the altar. You may want to complement that with a similar single candle stand at the end of several rows. You can have the candles lit by a pair of acolytes or ushers before the ceremony, or have each attendant carry a candle down the aisle to make a dramatic entrance.

If you're someone who likes symbolism as well as beauty in a ceremony, you may want to start by having a lit candle on both the bride's and groom's side, with a single unlit candle in the center. Once pronounced husband and wife, you each take your respective candles and, with their flames blending together, light the unity candle, joining your lives as one.

Be sure to check with proper church authorities regarding fire regulations that affect the location and number of candles you may have. Before the ceremony double check to see that all candles are securely placed in their holders.

Sharing of the Cup

A cup of wine (or other beverage) is symbolic of the cup of life. Both bride and groom drink from the same cup, which symbolizes their commitment to share all that the future may bring. All the sweetness life's cup may hold for you should be sweeter because you drink it together; whatever bitterness it may contain should be less bitter because you share them together.

Presentation of Roses

The presentation of roses (or other gifts) by the bride and groom to their parents symbolizes their affection and appreciation for the love which has brought them to this day. Together the couple presents roses to the groom's parents and then to the bride's parents, uniting the families in this joyous celebration. Surprise them by keeping this part of the ceremony a secret until this moment.

WRITING YOUR OWN VOWS

On the following pages are two examples of wedding ceremonies which can be used to help create your own. Whether you want to write a completely new ceremony, or simply add personal touches to an established one, these should give you some ideas. Individual sentences may be selected or you can combine the two ceremonies in any number of ways to best express your love and feelings for each other. Also included is a poem from *The Prophet* by Kahlil Gibran which is often read at some point in the main body of the ceremony. Another popular reading you may want to consider is "The Song of Songs" by Solomon in the Old Testament of the Bible.

Ideas

Here are some words or phrases you may want to include in your vows:

- love and comfort.
- pledge, promise, or commit.
- respect and cherish.
- share all life has to offer.
- share my life in good times and in bad.
- share with you life's sorrows and joys.

- I promise to share with you all my love.
- I promise to accept and love you.
- I promise to love and comfort you.
- I promise to be forever faithful.
- from this day forward.
- until the end of my life.
- until death do us part.

Poem from *The Prophet*
by Kahlil Gibran

On Marriage

Then Almitra spoke again and said, And what of Marriage, master?

And he answered saying:

You were born together, and together you shall be forevermore.

You shall be together when the white wings of death scatter your days.

Ay, you shall be together even in the silent memory of God.

But let there be spaces in your togetherness,
And let the winds of the heavens dance between you.

Love one another, but make not a bond of love:
Let it rather be a moving sea between the shores of your souls.

Fill each other's cup but drink not from one cup.

Give one another of your bread but eat not from the same loaf.

Sing and dance together and be joyous, but let each one of you be alone.

Even as the strings of a lute are alone
though they quiver with the same music.

Give your hearts, but not into each other's keeping.

For only the hand of Life can contain your hearts.

And stand together yet not too near togetherness:

For the pillars of the temple stand apart,
And the oak tree and the cypress grow not in each other's shadow.

SAMPLE CEREMONY

EXAMPLE ONE

Introduction

To all the family and friends of *Bride's name* and *Groom's name,* I welcome you here today, to share with us, as they pledge the vows of marriage which will unite them in Holy Matrimony. Let us join in our love and support of *Bride's name* and *Groom's name* as we bless the newlyweds by our prayers for their everlasting happiness.

Main Body

Marriage is one of the most important obligations that any two people commit to in their lifetime. Marriage offers the greatest challenges to overcome, but in return, marriage gives us love, strength and support from one another. It is the couple who perseveres and demonstrates unrelenting patience and faith who obtains the highest form of happiness within their marriage.

A good marriage is dependent upon many factors, but the first prerequisite is a strong bond of friendship and respect for one another. Your love for each other will grow deeper with the passing of each day, but genuine liking for each other, the willingness to accept each other's strong and weak points with understanding and respect, is the foundation for a strong marriage.

Introduction to the vows

The vows which you are about to exchange serve as a verbal representation of the love you pledge to each other. For it is not the words which you will speak today which will bond you together as one, but it is the inner sense of love and commitment that each of you feels within your soul.

[These can be repeated after the officiant or spoken directly between one another by changing the wording of the paragraph.]

(Officiant to the couple)

(Groom's/Bride's name) do you take *(Bride's/Groom's name)* to be your wedded *wife/husband?* Will you love *her/him,* comfort *her/him* honor *her/him* and respect *her/him?* Will you share all life has to offer, your hopes and dreams, your achievements and disappointments with *her/him* from this day forward?

I will.

Exchanging of the Rings

Heavenly Father, as we are gathered here today in celebration of the marriage of *Bride's name* and *Groom's name* we ask that you bless these rings, and may their marriage be blessed with peace, love and prosperity in all things.

[These words are repeated by the officiant as the rings are placed on both of their third fingers, with the groom going first, followed by the bride.]

With this ring, I thee wed, and offer a symbol of our everlasting love.

Closing of the Ceremony

By virtue of the authority vested in me, and in conformity with the laws of the state of *name of the state,* I pronounce you Husband and Wife. May you live together in blissful happiness from this day forward. You may kiss the bride.

SAMPLE CEREMONY

EXAMPLE TWO

Introduction

Dear family and friends, we have gathered here today to joyfully acknowledge the wedding of *Bride's name* and *Groom's name*. They have requested your presence on this memorable occasion in order that you might share with them the pledging of their everlasting love on this day of commitment. Let us pray in silence as we wish them all the happiness in their new life together.

Main Body

The commitment of marriage is one of the most important decisions two people will make in their lives. The vow of marriage is a pledge of their everlasting love uniting them in Holy Matrimony, whereby they commit to share all life has to offer, the good times and the bad, with patience and understanding. For a marriage to remain strong your faith must never waiver due to the trials and tribulations of everyday life. Remember, that the power of faith can conquer all obstacles.

A strong marriage is dependent upon many factors. Beyond the love and respect you share for one another, there must be a strong sense of commitment and loyalty that bonds you, and above all a true friendship and willingness to communicate with one another. A genuine liking for each other, the willingness to accept and understand each other's strengths and weaknesses is the foundation for a successful marriage.

Introduction to the Vows

Today as you exchange the vows of marriage which unite you as husband and wife, let us reflect upon just what a vow is. By definition, a vow is a solemn promise or pledge that binds one to perform a specified act; a formal declaration of such a promise or pledge. The vows pledged today are a formal and public announcement of your deep and devoted love and commitment to each other.

[These can be repeated after the officiant or spoken directly between one another by changing the wording of the paragraph.]

I, *Groom's/Bride's name* promise to you, *Bride's/Groom's name,* to share with you all of my love and my life in good times and in bad, to respect and to cherish you as my *wife/husband* from this day forward. Nothing shall become more important than our love for each other.

Exchanging of the Rings

The wedding ring is an unbroken circle which symbolizes unending and everlasting love and is a visible symbol which represents your inner commitment to one another. May your life together be blessed with everlasting happiness.

[These words are repeated after the officiant as the rings are placed on both their third fingers, with the groom going first, followed by the bride.]

As I place this ring upon your hand, may our separate lives become one as we commit our everlasting love to each other.

Closing the Ceremony

With the blessings of all the family and friends who are present, under the authority vested in me by this state, and in the name of the Holy Spirit, I now pronounce you Husband and Wife. You may kiss the bride.

The ceremony may end with the officiant saying: "May I present to you *Bride's name* and *Groom's full name*."

CEREMONY WORDING AND IDEAS WORKSHEET

PRELUDE: _____

_____

PROCESSIONAL: (Participants order) _____

_____

_____

WELCOME OR CALL TO WORSHIP: _____

_____

_____

READINGS OR PRAYER: _____

_____

_____

MUSIC (optional): _____

_____

WEDDING MEDITATION (Additional comments on marriage, optional): _____

_____

_____

_____

DECLARATION OF CONSENT (Directed to bride's father, or both sets of parents): _____

_____

_____

_____

READINGS OR PRAYER (Optional): _____

_____

_____

INTRODUCTION TO THE VOWS: _____

_____

_____

_____

_____

BRIDE'S VOWS: _____

_____

_____

Your Wedding Ceremony

GROOM'S VOWS: _____

_____

_____

AFFIRMATION BY GUESTS: _____

_____

EXCHANGE OF RINGS: _____

_____

_____

_____

BLESSING OF THE RINGS (Optional): _____

_____

PRONOUNCEMENT OF THE UNION: _____

_____

_____

MUSIC (optional): _____

_____

RECOGNITION OF THE CHILDREN (see Chapter on Second Marriages for ideas, optional): _____

_____

PRAYER OF HOPE OR LORD'S PRAYER (optional): _____

_____

SPECIAL ACTS OF CELEBRATION (lighting of the Unity Candle, Sharing of the Cup, Presentation of Roses or other symbolic celebration, optional): _____

_____

_____

BENEDICTION AND BLESSING: _____

_____

PRESENTATION OF THE NEW COUPLE: _____

_____

RECESSIONAL: _____

_____

_____

_____

_____

Notes

_____
_____
_____
_____
_____
_____
_____
_____
_____
_____
_____
_____
_____
_____
_____
_____
_____
_____
_____
_____
_____
_____
_____
_____
_____

CHAPTER FIVE

The Wedding Budget

In order to insure a well-planned wedding, determine a budget, or at least a basic starting figure. Most of the decisions you will need to make, such as the number of guests, type of food and beverages served will be determined by your budget.

DETERMINING YOUR BUDGET

In planning your expenses, recognize that you will probably have to compromise or change your budget along the way, unless you are one of the few who has an unlimited budget. Therefore, it is best to now plan a tentative budget by determining what you will need, who is paying for each item, and what you think it will cost.

This is the time to consider certain alternatives or compromises necessary to work within your budget. Remember that comparison shopping, creative ideas, and above all, organized planning can create a perfect wedding no matter what size the budget. Along with personal preferences, type and style of your wedding may be determined by your budget. If you have always dreamed of an elaborate, formal wedding, you may have to cut the guest list down. On the other hand, if you want all your family and friends to share your special day, expenses may require that you plan a lovely informal wedding, possibly a summer afternoon in the garden.

WHO PAYS FOR WHAT

There are no absolute rules on who pays for what. Traditionally, the majority of the wedding expenses have been borne by the bride's family. However, today with the increased cost of weddings, this obligation depends on the individual situation.

It may simply be determined by who is most willing and financially able to pay for the expense, or on who may be inviting the majority of guests. It is best to discuss the subject with both families in order to work out the best solution for everyone. Actually in today's world, couples who are older and financially able are often paying for their own, or part of their own, weddings.

NEW WAYS TO DIVIDE THE EXPENSES

The following are a few ideas on how costs are being divided, with the varying situations and circumstances of weddings today.

- **Bride and groom pay for the entire wedding**. Today more brides and grooms are paying for their own weddings, especially among older couples and when second marriages are involved.

- **Expenses shared by all**. Another alternative is to divide the entire cost of the wedding in thirds; the bride's family, groom's family, and couple each pay one-third.

- **Split expenses between bride's and groom's families**. The traditional expenses normally paid by each side can be combined,

then one-half paid by each family. The bride and groom would still be responsible for their own traditional expenses.

- **Assign various expenses**. One example may be when the bride's family pays for all ceremony costs, and the groom's family pays all reception costs. Another option may be to specify individual costs that each family pays. The bride's family may pay for the ceremony cost and reception food while the groom's family picks up the cost of flowers, liquor and music. They each pay for their own photographs. Certain expenses can also be assigned to the bride and groom, reducing the financial obligation of the parents. To make things easier, have the bills sent directly to the responsible party.

- **Each pays for their own guests**. This can be handled a few ways. All expenses for the ceremony and reception can be added together, to arrive at a per-person cost; then both sets of parents pay for their respective guests. Or, they each may pay for their traditional expenses, along with the per-guest cost of their invitees.

- **Groom's family pays for the entire wedding**. This scenario, although not the norm in the United States, is often used when a bride's family is deceased or when it's the groom's first marriage and the bride's second. A bride's family doesn't usually host a second wedding, and many times the groom's parents will want to host an elaborate event to celebrate the marriage of their son with their family and friends.

- **Divorced parents**. When the bride's parents are divorced, some of the above examples can be used as guidelines to determine who will pay for what. The wedding expenses can be paid for by the father, the mother, or they may each pay a portion, depending on their financial ability. Many times the wedding is hosted by the parent who raised the child.

The Wedding Budget

INCLUDING THE GROOM'S FAMILY

This may be determined by the extent to which the groom's family is financially participating in the wedding. The more they are contributing to various costs, the more input they should have in the planning or decisions in those areas.

The groom, *never* the bride, should be the one to approach his parents with regard to sharing expenses. Many parents don't realize this is becoming more acceptable. Some grooms' parents may offer to help finance the wedding right from the start. The final decision whether to accept this offer, and possibly give up some of the control, lies with the bride's parents (or the couple, if they have planned to host the wedding themselves). If the bride's family still prefers to host the celebration on its own, they may suggest the groom's parents host a subsequent reception to which a majority of their friends would be invited.

When both sets of parents are hosting the celebration, you should consider including the groom's parents on the wedding invitation (see the invitation section). Other ways to include them would be to have family members read a poem or scripture, include them in a unity candle lighting ceremony, or make them part of the processional.

KEEPING GOOD FINANCIAL RECORDS

To enable you to know where you stand in relationship to your overall budget, it is essential to keep accurate records during your planning. The worksheets provided in this wedding guide will help you keep track of what you ordered, the total price, the deposit given and the balance that is due. Take this wedding planner with you when shopping to immediately record information. Staying organized will prevent you from losing

monetary control and facing unpleasant last-minute surprises.

TRADITIONAL EXPENSES PAID BY

Traditionally, the expenses involved are paid for by the bride, the groom, and their families as follows:

Bride
- ☑ Wedding ring for the groom.
- ❑ A wedding gift for the groom.
- ❑ Gifts for the bridal attendants.
- ❑ Personal stationery.
- ❑ Medical examination and blood test.
- ❑ Accommodations for out-of-town attendants.

Groom
- ☑ The bride's engagement and wedding rings.
- ❑ A wedding gift for the bride.
- ❑ Gifts for the best man and ushers.
- ☑ Groom's wedding attire.
- ❑ Bride's bouquet and going away corsage.
- ❑ Mothers' corsages
- ❑ Boutonnieres for attendants and fathers.
- ❑ Medical examination and blood test.
- ☑ Marriage license.
- ❑ Clergyman's fee.
- ❑ The honeymoon expenses.
- ❑ Bachelor dinner (if not given by the best man, optional).

Bride's Family
- ❑ Engagement party (optional).
- ❑ Ceremony cost: location, music, rentals, and all related expenses.
- ❑ Entire cost of reception: food, beverage, entertainment, rental items, decorations, wedding cake.

❏ Bride's wedding attire and accessories.

❏ A wedding gift for the couple.

❏ Wedding invitations, announcements, and mailing costs.

❏ Bridesmaids' bouquets.

❏ Transportation for bridal party from bride's home to the site of ceremony.

❏ Bridesmaids' luncheon.

❏ Photography (groom's parents may pay for the pictures they would like).

❏ Personal wedding attire.

❏ Floral decorations.

❏ Special item they may wish to purchase. , toasting goblets, ring pillow, etc.

Groom's Family

❏ Rehearsal dinner party.

❏ Personal wedding attire.

❏ Travel and accommodations for groom's family.

❏ Wedding gift for the bride and groom.

❏ Special item they may wish to purchase, toasting goblets, ring pillow, etc.

❏ Any general expenses they may wish to contribute.

Attendants

❏ Wedding attire for themselves.

❏ Any travel expenses.

❏ Wedding gift for bride and groom.

❏ Showers given by maid of honor or bridesmaids.

❏ Bachelor party given by best man or ushers.

Bride and Groom

❏ Gifts of appreciation for parents or others who helped with your wedding.

❏ Expenses of items desired which have exceeded original budget allocations.

Optional Expenses

❏ Attendants' dresses are traditionally bought by each bridesmaid, but may be purchased by the bride or her family.

❏ Bridesmaids' luncheon is generally given by the bride's family; may be given by the bride.

❏ Bride's bouquet has traditionally been a gift from the groom, but may be purchased by the bride's family, along with the other flowers.

❏ Corsages for mothers and grandmothers have been the responsibility of the groom; the bride may opt to pay for her own mother's and grandmothers' corsages, or the bride's family may pay for them all.

❏ Rehearsal dinner is usually hosted by the groom's family, but it may be hosted by the bride's family or a close friend.

MONEY SAVING TIPS

The following are some ideas to help you keep your budget in line.

Wedding Attire

• Buy a ready-to-wear ankle or tea length dress that needs no alterations.

• Buy your wedding dress on sale or purchase a sample or discontinued line. (Many stores sell these at the end of the season.)

• Order your and the bridesmaids' dresses from a catalogue. These prices can be very reasonable; make sure you order early.

• Buy a gown from a girl whose wedding was cancelled. Check newspapers, consignment shops and bridal salons.

• See if the dress style you like can be made in a less expensive fabric, like a beautiful polyester blend rather than silk or taffeta.

The Wedding Budget

- Buy a dress that may be cut off or worn again.

- Borrow shoes from a friend.

- Buy shoes you can dye another color and wear again.

- Order the men's formal wear at a shop that provides the groom's tux free, or at a discount.

Accessories

- Make your own bridal purse. It can be done easily with a draw string.

- Make your own garter. Cover elastic with satin fabric and trim with lace.

- Make or borrow a ring pillow.

- Borrow or rent a cake knife and serving set.

- Borrow toasting glasses or purchase them through the mail.

- Borrow a cake top or decorate with fresh flowers.

Invitations

- Invitations can be much cheaper when ordered by mail.

- Buy pre-packaged cards; use stationery and handwrite each guest's invitation.

- Include the reception information on the ceremony invitation, and do not include separate response cards.

- Order invitations that will require only one stamp.

Receptions

- Have the reception in your or a friend's home or backyard.

- Reduce the size of your guest list.

- Decide on a morning or an afternoon reception, since it can usually be done for less money.

- Serve punch and cake or cocktails and hors d'oeuvres in the afternoon, rather than a luncheon or dinner.

- Prepare the food yourself with the help of friends, and serve it buffet style.

- Borrow items like punch bowl, serving dishes, and coffee pot instead of renting them.

- Buy food and liquor from wholesalers.

- Serve chicken or pasta; it's less expensive.

- Use paper plates, along with plastic cups and utensils, rather than renting china, glasses and silverware.

- Have friends or relatives bartend and help with the setup of tables.

- Instead of an open bar, arrange for tray service.

- Check hotel and restaurant management schools in your area for waiters, bartenders, and help with food preparation.

- Check culinary and bakery schools in your area. Many will prepare the food for its cost.

- Gratuity is paid only on food and liquor, not on the banquet hall.

Flowers and Decorations

- Carry a small bouquet or one flower, and have the attendants do the same.

- Use cut flowers which are common and in season, or decorate with potted plants or flowers in pretty baskets.

- Do your own floral arrangements and decorating. Get friends to help and do it the day before the wedding.

- Use one flower in a bud vase as centerpieces for the tables.

- Buy silk flowers and arrange them yourself. They can be used in your new home or given away as gifts.

- Celebrate outdoors, and take advantage of the natural foliage.

- Carry wildflowers, which can be tied together with colorful satin ribbons, and have the attendants carry the same.

- Use the same floral arrangements for both the ceremony and reception when they are in the same location. Table arrangements can be used to line the aisle, or may be grouped to appear as a single larger arrangement on each side of the altar.

- Check for floral schools in your area. Many will have students make the arrangements for the cost of the materials.

- Make your own decorations. You can get ideas from craft shops.

- Install twinkle lights yourself, and rent equipment to fill helium balloons rather than having a florist do this.

Music

- Have a friend play the organ, guitar, or harp for the ceremony.

- Have a friend sing the songs for the ceremony.

- For the reception keep the musicians to a minimum. Only have them play a couple of hours.

- Use taped music with a friend as the disc jockey.

Photographs

- Hire a professional photographer to shoot the main wedding photographs and order the smallest package. Have friends take candid pictures throughout the day.

- Have a friend who has good equipment and is an experienced photographer take all the wedding pictures.

- Check for a school which has advanced photography classes. Many experienced students will take the pictures for a flat fee and give you the negatives. Have the prints made by discount film houses.

The Wedding Budget

WEDDING EXPENSE RECORD

WEDDING ITEMS & SERVICES	TOTAL COST (cost to be paid by)				DEPOSIT PAID	BALANCE DUE
	Bride's Family	Groom's Family	Bride	Groom		
Ceremony						
Site Fee						
Marriage License						
Officiant's Fee						
Ceremony Music						
Other						
Bridal Consultant						
Stationery						
Invitations						
Reception Cards						
Response Cards						
Announcements						
Thank-you Notes						
Programs/Napkins						
Wedding Attire						
Bridal Dress						
Headpiece/Accessories						
Groom's Formal Wear						
Bride's Attendants						
Groom's Attendants						
Other						
Rings						
Engagement Ring						
Bride's Wedding Ring						
Groom's Wedding Ring						
Gifts						
Bride's gift						
Groom's gift						
Bridal Attendants						

WEDDING EXPENSE RECORD

WEDDING ITEMS & SERVICES	TOTAL COST (cost to be paid by)				DEPOSIT PAID	BALANCE DUE
	Bride's Family	Groom's Family	Bride	Groom		
Flowers						
Ceremony Site						
Reception Site						
Bride's flowers						
Bridesmaids' Bouquets						
Men's Boutonnieres						
Mothers/Grandmothers						
Reception						
Site Fee						
Caterer						
Liquor/Beverage						
Equipment						
Cake						
Music						
Photography						
Formal Portrait						
Parents' Albums						
Extra Pictures						
Videography						
Transportation						
Limousines, etc.						
Parking Attendants						
Parties						
Engagement						
Bridesmaids' luncheon						
Bachelor's Party						
Rehearsal Dinner						
Honeymoon						
Prenuptial Agreement						

CHAPTER SIX

Contracts and Consumer Fraud

Once you've interviewed and narrowed down the various professionals who will be providing all the services for your wedding, it will be time to firm up the details. With each professional, get a contract or letter of agreement describing the details of merchandise or service he or she is to provide. Having a contract will give you and the service provider peace of mind as the wedding day approaches. Having the details in writing will help ensure there are no misunderstandings. Or, if something should go wrong, you have the written contract to help renegotiate the price or provide evidence in case of litigation.

CONTRACTS

Most wedding professionals who provide goods and services will have standard contracts; if they don't, they can write the details out in a letter of agreement. The contract or agreement should include the costs, and should be signed by both parties.

Have contracts with:

You should have contracts or letters of agreement with the following professionals, or anyone else providing services for your wedding.

• Baker
• Bridal consultant
• Bridal salon
• Caterer
• Ceremony location
• Florist
• Musicians
• Photographer
• Reception hall
• Rental equipment company
• Stationery provider
• Transportation service
• Tuxedo rental store

CONTRACT TIPS

Write out all details. Specify all the details, from the size and type of flowers in your bouquet to the appropriate dress and number of breaks the musicians will take. The following list contains some of the general items that should be included in your contract.

• Day, date and time.
• Delivery dates, times and locations.
• Detailed list of merchandise ordered.
• List of services to be provided, number of hours, breaks, etc.
• Appropriate dress.
• Name of person in charge of your wedding.
• Alternative merchandise or service, if needed.
• Deposits or payment schedules.
• Last date to make changes or provide final guest count.
• Cancellation and refund policy.

Read and understand the contract. Read the contract carefully, especially the fine print. Make sure you understand and agree to everything; if not, ask questions or make changes—now's the time! Don't overlook the refund or cancellation policy.

Date and sign the contract. Make sure both parties sign and date the contract. You won't have a valid contract if the party promising to provide the merchandise or service doesn't sign it. This may only become an issue if something goes wrong, but then it may be too late.

Use credit cards. Put your deposit on a credit card. Pay the smallest deposit you can, and put it on a credit card. Putting all deposits and purchases on a credit card is the best way to protect yourself as a consumer. Special federal consumer protection laws protect all payments made with credit cards. You, as a consumer, have recourse to your credit card companies if you receive merchandise or services that do not live up to those you contracted for. You must first make an effort to correct the problem with the provider, or renegotiate the terms or price (do this in writing and keep copies). If this does not prove satisfactory, send a copy of your contract, correspondence, a letter explaining the problem, and pictures or any proof that will strengthen your case to your credit card company. If, after their investigation, they find the merchant did not live up to the terms of your contract, they will not release funds to his or her account (or will deduct them from the account) and will credit your account. If the retailer wishes to dispute this, he or she will have to file a claim against you for payment.

Avoid large cancellation fees. Read the fine print of the contract or ask exactly what the cancellation policy is. Will the deposit be refunded if you cancel six months in advance, or if the provider is able to re-book the date with another wedding? Does the contract state that, if the wedding is canceled, you are liable for 50% of the cost or for the total cost of the wedding, even if the original deposit was for much less than that cost?

Last minute cancellation fees are understandable and fair; just beware of what you are agreeing to before signing the contract. In the event you do have to cancel, notify all services as soon as possible.

WEDDING INSURANCE

Now you can protect what you have invested in your wedding day with Weddingsurance, offered by Fireman's Fund. You may find this insurance to be a small price to pay for peace of mind. The company has a variety of plans available that offer coverage and protection against wedding cancellations (they don't cover change of heart). They may include wedding photographs, wedding attire, personal liability and more. Contact Weddingsurance for information on reimbursement policy and restrictions. For an application or more information, write to Weddingsurance, 55 East Monroe Street, Suite 3300, Chicago, IL 60603. Or call 1-800-364-2433.

TIPS TO AVOID WEDDING RIP-OFFS

Unfortunately, as in almost any business, there are a few unscrupulous people out there who ruin the reputation for others in the wedding industry. Hopefully, after reading the following tips and advice, you will be a more aware consumer by knowing what the pitfalls are, and the ways consumers can be cheated or misled. If you deal with reputable services, get everything written in a contract and don't assume anything, you probably won't have a problem.

Wedding Attire

- Order your gown from a reputable salon, one you know will be there, and have your gown for your wedding date.

- Have the style number, dress size and color ordered written on the receipt, along with the deposit amount and promised delivery date.

- Order your gown in plenty of time, to allow any possible mistakes to be rectified before that all-important day.

- A couple of weeks after the gown is ordered, call to verify that the order has been placed with the manufacturer, and confirm a delivery date.

- Stay in touch with the salon periodically. Some salons have been known to close their doors after taking deposits from brides. They may not have ordered the dress or did not make any arrangements for the bride to take delivery of her gown. You don't need a last minute surprise like that!

- To find a reputable salon get recommendations from friends or names from bridal magazines.

- Be careful of hotel sales: Never pay the full price for a gown unless you are leaving with it in hand.

- With discontinued or sample sale gowns, check them carefully for irreparable damage or stains.

- When ordering a gown, be sure you are measured properly with a cloth tape, then ask to see the manufacturer's size charts and order the size according to your largest measurement. This will help minimize costly, unnecessary alterations. Remember it's better to order the dress a little larger than too small. And don't order a dress two sizes smaller than you wear, based on the idea of losing 20 pounds. If you don't lose it, you're in real trouble.

- Pay the smallest deposit you can, and put your deposit on a credit card. If you have a problem, you can dispute the charges, and often have the disputed charges taken off your bill.

- Make sure your contract or receipt includes a cancellation clause, stating the deposit will be refunded if the gown ordered does not arrive in good condition by the desired date.

- If the gown does not arrive on time as ordered, and your deposit was not refunded, consider taking the salon to small claims court.

- Report any fraudulent dealings to the Better Business Bureau, in hopes of preventing the same thing from happening to another bride

- Be cautious when ordering your dress at a discount over the phone, or by mail. Some of the problems that can arise are: not getting the style, color or size dress you ordered; getting a knock-off, or cheaper version of the dress you saw in the picture; running a greater chance of not getting your dress on time. Since you will be dealing with these problems long distance, and you've already paid them all the money in advance, it is not as easy to get problems resolved. You will also have to make your own arrangements for alterations and pressing. Weigh the cost savings, and the advantages and disadvantages of ordering from a discounter with whom you have no relationship, versus a full service salon which will handle any problems at their expense. Don't forget about shipping charges and long distance calls. The charges can add up, especially if there should be a problem.

Music

- Be aware that many bands either break up or change musicians, so the band you heard and booked eight months ago may not be the same group of musicians that will show up on your wedding day.

- Deal with an agent or the band leader. Specify the names of individual musicians you want to play or sing, and have their names written on the contract stating they will appear in person on that date. To be safe, have them sign it personally, when possible.

- Always get a contract that specifies the date, the location, and time the band or disc jockey should arrive, the number of hours they will play, the number of breaks they will take, the cost and overtime charges. List the names of the individual band members and specify the appropriate attire for the musicians or disc jockey.

Reception Sites

- Booking receptions too close together is another common problem that can occur. When another wedding is booked for the same day in the same room as yours, make sure you specify your exact time, from which hour to which hour, allowing enough time for clean-up. If you feel the catering manager or reception coordinator has not allowed enough time for clean-up or over-staying by those attending the first reception, point this out. You don't want your guests to arrive and have to wait in the wings. Remember the more weddings the managers book, the more money they make, and sometimes they try to squeeze too many in on the same day.

- Cancellation policies. Make sure you read the fine print and fully understand the cancellation policy. Are you liable for 50% of the entire reception cost, or just the small deposit you made, if you cancel months before the wedding? What if you cancel at the last minute? Do you get your deposit back if they are able to rebook the room? Check these things out. Put your deposit on a credit card; you will have a better chance of having it refunded in case there's a dispute.

- Avoid hidden extras by reading the fine print of the contract. If the contract doesn't specify certain fees such as set-up, clean-up, overtime fees or gratuities, ask about them. Inquire about charges for cake cutting, coat check and corkage fees. Itemize all the costs; then state on the contract no additional fees are to be added. If anything should change, initial and date the new charge.

- Determine the last date on which you can give the caterer or banquet manager your final guest count. Have them base the costs on a per-person basis, and charge you only for those guests who will be actually attending, not for the number of guests you originally invited.

- With your caterer, specify in writing the exact menu items that are to be served. Some caterers have been known to substitute less expensive food items than those you originally contracted for. Don't pay 100% of the total bill in advance; hold something out until the reception is over.

Jewelers

You need to be as cautious when buying an engagement ring as you are when making any major purchase. This is an area in which it is easy to be misled. Most people don't know much about diamonds, and today imitation stones look so real to a novice's naked eye.

- Be cautious of jewelers who send you to a friend who is an appraiser. Sometimes they work in teams to defraud customers. Take the stone to an independent jewelry appraiser or to another jewelry store.

- Be careful of a "great deal." It may be just that – a great deal – but for whom? The old adage, "If it looks too good to be true, it probably is," hasn't hung around all these years because there's nothing to it. One method of enticing people to buy quickly is to give them a discount, or declare "the sale ends today." Take your time, shop around, know what a stone of that size and quality should cost.

- Don't buy from discounters who don't have a permanent place of business. They may take your money and disappear, leaving you with a ring that is not what it was represented to be. And then what recourse do you have?

- Ask to look at the stone through the jeweler's loupe (small magnifying glass). Look for inclusions or other imperfections.

- If the stone is loose, turn the stone upside down and place it over a newspaper. If you can read the print through the stone, the stone is probably glass, and not a diamond.

- Purchase the stone on consignment, then have an independent appraisal done on it.

- Deal with a jeweler or shop that has a certified gemologist on staff, and one that is a member of the American Gem Society. If you feel you need to check them out more thoroughly, call the Better Business Bureau. It's no guarantee that they are above reproach, but it does guarantee that there have been no complaints filed against the jeweler or store, which is a start.

Photographers

- Pictures and your videotape will be the lasting memories you'll have long after the last piece of cake is eaten. Be sure to work with a professional who specializes in weddings, especially for shooting the ceremony.

- A friend or photographer may tell you that they have done other people's weddings and assure you they can handle yours. Be cautious; ask to see pictures from those weddings. Even if the price is "great," even free, think twice about it. Pictures may not seem so important now, but not having good wedding pictures may be something you may regret for years to come.

- Some photographers, who have a studio with other photographers working for them, book your wedding and lead you to believe they will be the one taking the pictures. The day arrives, and so does another photographer, someone you've never met. Specify in your contract the name of the person who will be taking the pictures. Look at pictures of weddings that person has shot (not the ones of the other studio photographers).

- Meet with the actual photographer who will be taking your pictures—at the wedding site, if possible. Discuss the type and number of shots, the length of time the photographer will be taking pictures and the appropriate dress.

- In the event that for some reason your photographs don't turn out, state in your contract that you are not obligated to purchase them, and that all deposits be refunded.

- Don't be lured into what you think is a great deal by committing to the lowest priced package, and then end up having to pay heavy prices for additional photos. Some photographers make the package deal sound cheap until they've completed the job. Ask ahead of time what the additional picture charge will be for 5x7s and 8x10s. If considering a package, really study the options to select the package that will most realistically cover all the shots you want of your wedding, and avoid the extra expensive "additional photos."

- If your contract with the photographer is for a specified number of hours, be sure to make prior agreement of what overtime charges will be in the event the reception runs longer than anticipated. You don't want the photographer to leave at the end of four hours, missing shots of cutting the cake or tossing the garter. Try not to be locked into a specified number of hours, with high overtime charges.

- Most photographers won't sell you the film or negatives of your wedding pictures. If you come across a photographer who offers to take your pictures for a set fee, and give you the film at the end of the reception, be cautious. Before

agreeing to do this, contact a professional lab and get the price of developing the film and having 5x7 or 8x10 prints made. You might find that with his fee, and the print costs, you would be paying a lot more for the pictures. Another drawback is that the photographer is probably going to want to get paid when he hands over the film, before you have seen the quality of the shots. You have no guarantees of what you're going to get, and he has no incentive to take the best shots or correct problems, since you may never see him again after the reception. If you choose to go this route, don't agree to pay in full until after you have had the film developed. And state in your contract that if the pictures don't turn out, you owe nothing.

Flowers

- To avoid disappointment with your flowers, in your contract specify the type and number of flowers to be used in the bouquets and table arrangements. List flowers which can be substituted in the event your first choice is not available. Specify price adjustments if less expensive flowers are substituted.

- Give your florist pictures of bouquets and arrangements similar to what you want. In your contract specify details like the sizes and colors of the arrangements and bouquets. The pictures will ensure the florist has an idea of what you want. Make provisions to adjust the balance due, if the arrangements are smaller than you contracted for, or if they are not fresh.

CHAPTER SEVEN

Invitations and Stationery

Your invitation makes the first impression! It sets the tone and should reflect the style of wedding you are having. So choose your invitation and other stationery to reflect the same importance you place on the rest of your wedding. Make them special.

Today there are many exciting things to choose from, everything from the very traditional to informal and unique custom designs. Prices will vary, so shop around. There is a wide variety in types of paper; the traditional thick white or ivory, a less formal pastel parchment with colored printing, or you may select a moire or pearlized paper. Add a ribbon or your monogram for that unique custom touch.

Tradition has established guidelines for wording invitations, although today many variations are being used. However, the general information remains the same. Once the wording is determined, the size and style of the lettering is selected from a wide variety available.

Don't forget when selecting, that oversized or heavy invitations will require more postage. Start looking early, with the wide variety available you'll find just the right one for your wedding. The most important thing is that your guests receive the message with the warmth and happiness with which it was sent.

THE GUEST LIST

Your invitations should be ordered about three months in advance. This allows plenty of time for delivery, addressing and mailing. They should be sent out four to six weeks before the date. So start everyone compiling their guest lists, along with addresses and phone numbers, early. Once the final budget and number of guests to be invited is determined, make one master list of those who are receiving invitations and of those receiving announcements. List them in alphabetical order to save time later.

Arriving at the number of guests.

There are a few things to consider when determining the number of guests to be invited.

• **Wedding Style**. Consider your personal preference and that of your fiancé; do you want a large gathering, with everyone you know there, or do you prefer to keep it small and intimate?

• **Your Budget**. Next consider the budget you're working with, and the type of party you want. Would you rather invite fewer guests to an elegant sitdown dinner with open bar, or be able to invite more people and have a less elaborate reception?

• **Space**. If you have your heart set on a location for the ceremony or reception, and space is a problem, this may be the determining factor in how many guests you can invite.

Dividing the Guest List

Usually each family invites half the guests. However, one family may have fewer guests if the wedding is away from their home town. When most of the bride's and groom's guests are the same, another alternative is to split the list in thirds. The couple provides one-third; the bride's family and the groom's family each provide a third. This may vary with each wedding. Determine what will work best for your individual situation. Try to avoid any hurt feelings.

As a general rule, about 20% to 25% of the guests invited will be unable to attend. If you were, for budget or space reasons, unable to invite all the guests you would have liked, then, as regrets are received, immediately send out other invitations. Send the first invitations early enough to allow you to receive responses and be able to get the other invitations out about three weeks before the wedding.

Who Gets Invitations

Invitations should not only be sent to the guests on the list, but also to your fiancé's immediate family, your wedding officiant, your wedding party, and their spouses or dates even though they have been invited informally. It makes for a nice memento.

Cutting Down the Guest List

Cutting down the guest list, although unpleasant and difficult, is a necessary reality. How do you do it, and where do you start?

Everyone may have to cut some persons from their lists, or perhaps the person with the largest list will have to do the majority of cutting. Start by eliminating certain categories of people; business or casual acquaintances, friends you haven't seen in ten years, friends who live long distances away, and children of friends. On invitations to friends with children, make no mention of the children and leave their names off the invitation, if you not wish them to attend. Have family members or close friends mention that you are unable to accommodate children.

It is not necessary to invite dates for single guests. However, if you do, send a separate invitation addressed to them, as long as you are sure who the guest will be.

Special Guests

If you are Catholic you may want to send an invitation to the Pope. These arrangements may be made with your priest, so check with him. A beautiful papal blessing will be sent to you, which can be framed and cherished forever.

No matter what religion you are you may want to send an invitation to the President of the United States at the White House in Washington, D.C. You will receive a beautiful response blessing your marriage and signed by the President and First Lady. This is a wonderful keepsake to have.

ORDERING INVITATIONS

Choose a stationer who offers a wide variety of styles and prices to select from, and one who is knowledgeable about wording and type styles. Determine the number to order by figuring one for each married couple, and couples who live together, one for each single person and another for his or her date, if invited. (Dates need not be invited, but if they are, they should receive a separate invitation.) A separate invitation is also sent to children who are sixteen or older. Don't forget to order an invitation for your officiant, attendants, their dates if invited, and both sets of parents. Order several extra invitations for keepsakes, for mistakes (unless you're perfect), and last minute invitees (how could you have forgotten Cousin Bertha?).

There are various types of printing processes used to print invitations, and they vary in price. Ask to see samples, and make your decision based on what you like and what fits your budget.

- Engraved invitations are the most traditional and formal of all, but also the most expensive. This is an old process whereby the paper is pressed onto a metal plate, causing the letters to be slightly raised on the paper.

- Thermography, a relatively new printing process that has grown in popularity, probably is the number one choice for invitations today. This is a process that fuses ink and powder together on the paper to create raised letters which resemble engraving. Since plates don't have to be made and the printing process is quicker, thermography is about half the price of engraved invitations.

- Offset printing is the least expensive of the three processes. This is the standard printing process where the ink lays flat on the paper. This is a less formal look, but there are many ink colors and type styles to select from.

Calligraphy has become increasingly popular over the last few years, due both to the new computerized machines which can produce it, and the growing formality of weddings. Calligraphy is an elegant old italic script, used primarily in the past to address envelopes. Now, with the new computerized calligraphy machines, which create a perfect script each time, invitations can easily be done also. Most machines found in stationery stores can only inscribe one or two invitations at a time, but it's certainly faster and less expensive than having them hand done by a calligrapher (still another option, of course).

Examples.

Outer Envelope:

Mr. and Mrs. Robert L. Coleman
1035 5th Avenue, Apartment 16
New York , New York 10016

Unsealed Inner Envelope:

Mr. and Mrs. Coleman
Susan and Michael
(when inviting children
under 16 years of age)

When a married woman keeps her maiden name, address her as "Miss" or "Ms." Her name can appear first, or the names can appear in alphabetical order. "Mrs." is only used when the married woman takes her husband's last name.

PROOFREADING YOUR INVITATION

Proofread your invitations and other stationery carefully, both when you place the order, and when you pick up the finished stationery. See if it's possible to check the wording and layout after the typesetting has been done, but before it is printed. Take your mother or a friend along to help you proofread. The following are some things to look for:

• Check the style and color to be sure you have what you ordered.

• Is the type style correct, and the right size?

• Are the names correctly spelled, with proper titles?

• Does it have the proper date and time of the wedding?

• Is the day, date, time and year written out? And are they all correct?

• Is the address correct?

• Are the words "honour" and "o'clock" written out correctly?

• Is the spacing proper; do the lines end where they should?

• Are there commas between the city and state?

• Are there periods after abbreviations?

• Are the proper words capitalized?

• Is the phone number correct, when included?

• Are the directions correct on direction enclosures?

WORDING INVITATIONS

Usually the parents of the bride issue the invitations and announcements. However, a close friend, relative, or the couple themselves, may issue the invitation. All names, no nicknames, the date and the time are written out in full; the year may be omitted if preferred. The traditional wording for a religious ceremony would read "the honour of your presence" and for a reception card would always read "the pleasure of your company." When requesting a response it may be written in any of the following ways: "R.S.V.P.," "Please respond," "Kindly respond," or "The favor of a reply is requested." The one sponsoring the wedding is not necessarily the one paying for it.

Traditional Invitation

> *Mr. and Mrs. Charles Smith*
> *request the honour of your presence*
> *at the marriage of their daughter*
> *Donna Marie*
> *to*
> *Mr. William Hunt Crain*
> *Saturday, the eighth of September*
> *Nineteen hundred and ninety-five*
> *at four o'clock*
> *First Presbyterian Church*
> *Santa Barbara, California*

Combined Ceremony and Reception Invitation

This example also includes the response or R.S.V.P. at the bottom. A separate response card could be sent in place of this, if you prefer.

> *Mr. and Mrs. Charles Smith*
> *request the honour of your presence*
> *at the marriage of their daughter*
> *Donna Marie*
> *to*
> *Mr. William Hunt Crain*
> *Saturday, the fifth of June*
> *Nineteen hundred and ninety-five*
> *at four o'clock*
> *First Presbyterian Church*
> *Santa Barbara, California*
> *Reception*
> *immediately following the ceremony*
> *Biltmore Hotel*
>
> *R.S.V.P.*
> *89 Lilac Lane*
> *Santa Barbara, California 93108*

One Remarried Parent Host

When the bride's remarried mother is the host. (This is an example without the year.)

> *Mr. and Mrs. Donald Ryan*
> *Request the honour of your presence*
> *at the marriage of her daughter*
> *Donna Marie Smith*
> *to*
> *Mr. William Hunt Crain*
> *Saturday, the fifth of June*
> *at four o'clock*
> *First Presbyterian Church*
> *Santa Barbara, California*

When the bride's remarried father hosts, it would read:

> *Mr. and Mrs. Charles Lee Smith*
> *request the honour of your presence*
> *at the marriage of his daughter*

One Divorced Unmarried Parent Hosts

When the bride's unmarried mother hosts, she uses her maiden and married name.

> *Mrs. Helen Johnson Smith*
> *requests the honour of your presence*
> *at the marriage of her daughter*
> *Donna Marie*
> *to*
> *Mr. William Hunt Crain*
> *Saturday, the fifth of June*
> *at four o'clock*
> *First Presbyterian Church*
> *Santa Barbara, California*

When the bride's unmarried father hosts.

> *Mr. Charles Lee Smith*
> *requests the honour of your presence*
> *at the marriage of his daughter*

Two Remarried Parents Host

If the bride's parents are divorced, and both remarried, but wish to co-host the wedding, the names should appear with the mother's name first.

> *Mr. and Mrs. Donald Ryan*
> *and*
> *Mr. and Mrs. Charles Smith*
> *request the honour of your presence*
> *at the marriage of*
> *Donna Marie Smith*
> *to*
> *Mr. William Hunt Crain*
> *Saturday, the fifth of June*
> *at four o'clock*
> *First Presbyterian Church*
> *Santa Barbara, California*

A Stepmother Hosts

When the bride's stepmother and father sponsor the wedding, the invitation can read as follows. This example would most commonly only be used if the stepmother raised the bride, or the bride's mother is deceased.

> *Mr. and Mrs. Charles Lee Smith*
> *request the honour of your presence*
> *at the marriage of Mrs. Smith's stepdaughter*
> *Donna Marie*
> *to*
> *Mr. William Hunt Crain*
> *Saturday, the fifth of June*
> *at four o'clock*
> *First Presbyterian Church*
> *Santa Barbara, California*

Divorced Unmarried Parents Co-Host

If the bride's parents are divorced and neither has remarried, the invitation may read:

> *Mrs. Helen Johnson Smith*
> *and*
> *Mr. Charles Lee Smith*
> *request the honour of your presence*
> *at the marriage of their daughter*
> *Donna Marie*
> *to*
> *Mr. William Hunt Crain*
> *Saturday, the fifth of June*
> *at four o'clock*
> *First Presbyterian Church*
> *Santa Barbara, California*

Invitations and Stationery

On an informal invitation, you may delete Mr. and Mrs.

> *Helen Johnson Smith*
> *and*
> *Charles Lee Smith*
> *request the honour of your presence*
> *at the marriage of their daughter*

Another option, depending on their relationship is:

> *Mr. and Mrs. Charles Lee Smith*
> *request the honour of your presence*
> *at the marriage of their daughter*

Groom's Parents Host

When the groom's family sponsors the wedding the invitation may read:

> *Mr. and Mrs. Richard Crain*
> *request the honour of your presence*
> *at the marriage of*
> *Donna Marie Smith*
> *to their son*
> *William Hunt Crain*
> *Saturday, the fifth of June*
> *at four o'clock*
> *First Presbyterian Church*
> *Santa Barbara, California*

Bride's and Groom's Parents Co-Host

> *Mr. and Mrs. Charles Smith*
> *and*
> *Mr. and Mrs. Richard Crain*
> *request the honour of your presence*
> *at the marriage of their children*
> *Donna Marie Smith*
> *and William Hunt Crain*
> *Saturday, the fifth of June*
> *at four o'clock*
> *First Presbyterian Church*
> *Santa Barbara, California*

Bride and Groom Host

When the bride and groom are sponsoring their own wedding, the traditional wording would be:

> *The honour of your presence*
> *is requested at the marriage of*
> *Donna Marie Smith*
> *to*
> *William Hunt Crain*
> *Saturday, the fifth of June*
> *at four o'clock*
> *First Presbyterian Church*
> *Santa Barbara, California*

CONTEMPORARY WORDING

The following are examples of some contemporary wording:

Bride's Parents Host

A less formal invitation sponsored by the bride's parents.

*We ask only those dearest in our hearts
to join us in celebrating the marriage
of our daughter Donna to Bill Crain
at four o'clock
July fifth nineteen eighty six
First Presbyterian Church
Santa Barbara, California
Helen and Charles Smith*

Bride and Groom Host

*We invite you to join us
in celebrating our love.
On this day we will marry the one
we laugh with, live for, dream with, love.
We have chosen to continue our growth
through marriage, please join
Donna Smith
and
Bill Crain
at four o'clock
Saturday, the fifth of July
First Presbyterian Church
Santa Barbara, California*

INVITATIONS FOR SECOND WEDDINGS

Bride's Parents Host

*Mr. and Mrs. Charles Smith
request the honour of your presence
at the marriage of their daughter
Donna Smith Wilson
to
Mr. William Hunt Crain
Saturday, the eighth of September
at four o'clock
First Presbyterian Church
Santa Barbara, California*

Bride and Groom Host

*The honour of your presence
is requested at the marriage of
Donna Smith Wilson
to
Mr. William Hunt Crain
Saturday, the eighth of September
at four o'clock
First Presbyterian Church
Santa Barbara, California*

Children Invite Guests to Marriage of Their Parents

> *Jamie and Jeff Adams*
> *and*
> *Lauren, Todd and Ashley Johnson*
> *request the honour of your presence*
> *at the marriage of their parents*
> *Janice Stewart Adams*
> *to*
> *Robert Lee Johnson*
> *Saturday, the fifth of June*
> *at four o'clock*
> *First Presbyterian Church*
> *Santa Barbara, California*

INVITATIONS TO REAFFIRMATIONS OF VOWS

Whether you have recently eloped, or it's your ten year anniversary and you are celebrating the reaffirmation of your wedding vows, invitations may be worded in this way:

> *The honour of your presence*
> *is requested at the reaffirmation*
> *of the wedding vows of*
> *Mr. and Mrs. Richard Rosengren*
> *Saturday, the twenty-eighth of May*
> *at four o'clock*
> *The Crystal Cathedral*
> *Santa Ana, California*
>
> *Reception to follow in*
> *the Church Hall.*

RECEPTION CARDS

One invitation will serve the purpose when all the guests are invited to both the ceremony and reception. However, when the ceremony and reception are held in different locations, you may enclose a reception card. Or when only a select number of guests are invited to the reception, a separate card is enclosed. It should be of the same paper and type style and is generally half the size. You may want to include directions or a map on the back. The following are examples of how the cards may read:

Informal Reception Card

A less formal reception card would read:

> *Reception*
> *immediately following the ceremony*
> *Biltmore Hotel*
> *13495 Cabrillo Blvd.*
> *Santa Barbara*

Formal Reception Card

A formal reception card to accompany a formal invitation.

> *Mr. and Mrs. Charles Smith*
> *request the pleasure of your company*
> *Saturday, the eighth of September*
> *at half past four o'clock*
> *Biltmore Hotel*
>
> *R.S.V.P.*
> *1438 Edgecliff Lane*
> *Santa Barbara, California*

RESPONSE CARD

When a response card is sent out, it should be accompanied by a self addressed, pre-stamped envelope. The following are some examples.

> *The favor of a reply is requested*
> *by the twenty-first day of May*
>
> M _____
>
> *will* _____*attend.*

or

> *Please respond on or before*
> *the twenty-first of May*
>
> M_____
>
> *will* _____*attend.*

TRADITIONAL PEW CARD

> *Catherine and Robert*
> *First Presbyterian Church*
> *Bride's Section*
> *Pew Number* _____

or

> M _____
> *First Presbyterian Church*
> *Bride's Section*
> *Pew Number* _____

INVITATION TO THE RECEPTION

If the ceremony is small or just for family members, and the reception guest list larger, invitations are issued to the reception, with ceremony cards enclosed. The invitation would read:

> *Mr. and Mrs. Charles Smith*
> *request the pleasure of your company*
> *at the wedding reception of their daughter*
> *Donna Marie*
> *and*
> *Mr. William Hunt Crain*
> *Saturday, the eighth of September*
> *at half past four o'clock*
> *Biltmore Hotel*
> *Santa Barbara, California*
>
> *Please respond*
> *1438 Edgecliff Lane*
> *Santa Barbara, California*

Formal Ceremony Card

> *Mr. and Mrs. Charles Smith*
> *request the honour of your presence*
> *Saturday, the eighth of September*
> *at four o'clock*
> *First Presbyterian Church*
> *Santa Barbara, California*

Informal Ceremony Card

> *Ceremony*
> *at four o'clock*
> *First Presbyterian Church*

Invitations and Stationery

ANNOUNCEMENTS

Announcements are sent to people who have not been invited to the wedding because of distance, people who are only acquaintances, or those you know would be unable to attend. An announcement does not require a gift. Therefore, it is a nice way to inform people of your marriage without obligating them.

Announcements may be sent by either or both sets of parents, or by the couple themselves. They are mailed the day of, or the day after, the ceremony, not before. The date is included, but not the time or location of the ceremony and reception.

Traditional Announcement

> *Mr. and Mrs. Charles Smith*
> *have the honour of announcing*
> *the marriage of their daughter*
> *Donna Marie*
> *and*
> *Mr. William Hunt Crain*
> *on Saturday, the eighth of September*
> *Nineteen hundred and ninety-five*
> *Santa Barbara, California*

ADDRESSING AND MAILING INVITATIONS

Your invitations should always be neatly hand written, never typed. If you don't have legible writing or enough time, you may recruit your mother or a bridesmaid, or you might hire a calligrapher. Calligraphy is always beautiful, but more costly.

The name, address, and don't forget the zip code, should appear on the outside envelope.

Having a return address printed on the envelope will save a lot of time and looks the nicest. If your invitation includes an inside envelope, repeat the names, and first names of young children that may be invited. Children over sixteen should receive their own invitations. For a single person, include the name "and guest" on the inside envelope; or, if you know the guest he or she intends to bring, a separate invitation should be sent. When two people live together, send one invitation addressed to both.

It is proper that formal titles, such as Doctor, Captain, and Reverend be written out. It is usual to abbreviate the following: Ms., Mrs. and Mr.

The invitation should be placed in the envelope with the engraved, or printed, side facing up. Extra enclosures such as pew cards, reception cards, or at-home cards may be placed next to the engraved side or be inserted in the fold, if any. The unsealed inner envelope is then placed in the outer envelope so that the guests' names are seen first when the envelope is opened. Weigh the invitation before mailing to ensure proper postage. Love stamps may also be purchased to send your invitation with that special touch.

RESERVED SECTION OR PEW CARDS

Pew cards are often used in very large weddings to invite special guests or close relatives to be seated toward the front, in the reserved section designated by ribbons.

The pew card may be hand written or engraved, saying: Bride's or Groom's section or "within the ribbons." The pew card is mailed after the guest has accepted the wedding invitation, and should be handed to the usher before they are seated.

THANK YOU NOTES

It is a good idea to order your thank you notes or other stationery at the same time as the invitations. You may choose a folded card with your name or monogram imprinted on the outside, a folded piece of stationery, or packaged thank-you cards. Make sure to order enough thank-you cards. Extras can always be used later. Send your thank-you note as soon as the gifts are received. It is not only courteous but prevents them from piling up. Sign your maiden, or first name only before the wedding and your married name after. It is always best to mention the gift; it sounds more personal, except in the case where money is sent. Don't mention the amount. You may want to tell them what you intend to purchase.

AT-HOME CARDS

These cards are optional, but should be ordered at the same time as the invitations or announcements. At-home cards are usually included with the announcement, or sent separately after the wedding. It's a nice way to inform your friends of your new address and let them know whether you're keeping your maiden name.

An example would be:

Mr. and Mrs. William Crain

or

Mr. William Crain *and* *Ms. Donna Smith* *after the ninth of September* *1684 San Vicente* *Brentwood, California*

OUT-OF-TOWN GUESTS

When guests are coming from out of town, especially from some distance, show your appreciation with a little extra hospitality. Offer to arrange accommodations at the home of a relative or friend, or at a hotel if they prefer. Try to spend time with them before the ceremony, because you may not get much of a chance afterward.

If they arrive a day or two before the wedding, have them help you with last minute errands. You may want to have a luncheon for them or include them in the rehearsal dinner party.

If you are expecting many close family members and friends from out of town that you don't get a chance to see often, consider giving yourselves one day to visit and relax before taking off on your honeymoon. It can be fun to get together the following day for brunch and to relive the wedding or open some gifts. I'm sure the extra time spent with you will be well appreciated.

INVITATION KEEPSAKES

There are a number of decorative ideas for your wedding invitation after the ceremony. Listed below are a few ideas to turn your invitation into a decorative keepsake.

- Have your invitation mounted and framed or displayed with your wedding bouquet in a shadow box. Either of these can be set on a table or hung on a wall in your new home.

- Have the wording of your invitation embroidered on the front of a small pillow. The wording can also be written on the pillow with fabric paint. The pillow can then be trimmed with lace and satin ribbons. Pillows are nicely displayed on a bed or in a display cabinet.

- Buy a beautiful crystal or silver box, which can be found in fine china stores, and have the wording of your invitation engraved on the lid. Either of these can be filled with potpourri or candy and displayed on a table in the living room of your new home.

- Have the wording of your invitation hand painted or silk screened on a porcelain plate. The plate can be displayed in a china cabinet, hung on a wall or put on a stand and placed on a table.

STATIONERY OVERVIEW

Thank You cards – small cards, usually folded, used to express your thanks for gifts received.

Invitations – order a few more than you think you'll need.

Reception cards – used when only a select number of the guests invited to the ceremony are also invited to the reception.

Ceremony cards – this card is enclosed when a select few guests are invited to the ceremony, in addition to the reception, to which all guests are invited.

Response cards – guests return this card with their names and whether they will be attending.

Pew cards – mainly used in large, formal weddings, they indicate special seating positions.

Rain cards – informs guests invited to an outdoor wedding, of an alternative location in case of rain.

Maps – small, printed maps with directions to the ceremony and/or reception site to aid guests in finding the location.

Travel cards – this card is used to inform guests of any special wedding day transportation you have arranged, such as a bus or trolley to take out-of-town guests from their hotel to the ceremony. The card can also be used to indicate parking locations, and whether fees or gratuities have been paid in advance.

Weekend Wedding Program – informs guests of the many activities scheduled for the weekend, and ideas of appropriate attire. Includes information on travel or lodging arrangements you may have made.

Ceremony Program – a program stating the order in which things will take place during the ceremony. It will list songs, prayers, and scriptures to be read, along with names of attendants, vocalist or organist.

At Home cards – these cards inform friends of your new address.

ADDRESSING TIPS

- **Address all wedding invitation envelopes by hand, or have them done by a calligrapher or a calligraphy machine**. Never use computer labels.

- **Don't abbreviate.** Spell out all streets, cities and states.

- **A woman with a military or professional title should be listed on a separate line, above her husband's name, on outer envelope.**

Doctor Diane Bartlet
Mr. David Bartlet

On inner envelope she is listed on the same line.

Doctor Bartlet and Mr. Bartlet

- **Send a person over sixteen years of age a separate wedding invitation.**

- **When two siblings over sixteen live together, send one invitation listing them alphabetically.**

- **When inviting children under sixteen, list titles and last names of parents on the inner envelope.** Just below those names, list first names of the invited children. Don't write "and Family".

Mr. and Mrs. Jones
Carol and Michael

- **When a woman keeps her maiden name, list her as "Miss" or" Ms."** "Mrs." is only used when she takes her husband's name. Both names are listed on the same line, and either name may be listed first.

MONEY SAVING TIPS

- **Order thermography, rather than engraved invitations**. Thermography is a raised letter printing process that looks similar to engraving, but is much less expensive.

- **Shop around**. Many people sell invitations out of their homes and offer discounts of 10 to 20%. Or you may find it cheaper to order through the mail. One word of caution: Proper invitation wording and layout is more difficult than you may think. It may be wiser to pay a little more and get the help of an experienced professional.

- **Use standard size invitations**. Stay away from over-sized invitations, or invitations that need to be mailed in a box or tube. Your mailing expenses will skyrocket.

- **Order more invitations**. Order a few more invitations than you think you'll need, because an additional 25 invitations are a lot less expensive than later having to place a reorder, for which you will be charged another set-up fee.

- **You may want to skip extra charges for envelope lining**.

- **Eliminate response cards**. Do not include separate response cards; include RSVP and phone number on the invitation. This will save the cost of the card, an additional envelope and the return stamp. It will make the invitation lighter, and can possibly avoid additional postage, also.

STATIONERY WORDING WORKSHEET

Type style _____ Color ink _____

INVITATIONS:

_____

_____

_____

_____

_____

_____

_____

_____

_____

_____

_____

_____

_____

_____

_____

_____

_____

_____

RETURN ADDRESS FOR ENVELOPE:

_____

_____

RECEPTION OR CEREMONY CARDS:

_____

_____

_____

_____

RESPONSE CARDS:

_____

_____

_____

_____

ADDRESS FOR RESPONSE CARDS:

_____

_____

_____

PEW CARDS:

_____

_____

_____

_____

ANNOUNCEMENTS:

_____

_____

_____

_____

_____

_____

_____

_____

_____

NAPKINS/MATCHBOOKS:

_____

_____

THANK YOU NOTES:

_____

_____

ADDRESS FOR THANK YOU NOTE envelope:

_____

_____

_____

Invitations and Stationery

STATIONERY WORKSHEET

	ESTIMATE #1		ESTIMATE #2	
	Name		Name	
	Phone		Phone	
	Description	Cost	Description	Cost
Wedding Invitations				
Number				
Printed Envelopes				
Envelope Liners				
Calligraphy				
Response Cards				
Printed Envelopes				
Announcement Cards				
Number				
Printed Envelopes				
At-Home Cards				
Number				
Printed Envelopes				
Thank-you Notes				
Number				
Printed Envelopes				
Miscellaneous				
Napkins				
Matchbooks				
Seating Place Cards				
Programs				
TOTAL				

STATIONER CHOICE

Name _____ Order Date/Deposit _____

Address _____ Pick-up Date _____

Phone/Salesperson _____ Balance Due _____

93

GUEST ACCOMMODATION LIST

Guest Name _____

Date/Time Arriving _____ Departing _____

Name of Hotel _____

Address/Phone _____

Type of Room/Rate _____

Reservation Date/Deposit _____

Guest Name _____

Date/Time Arriving _____ Departing _____

Name of Hotel _____

Address/Phone _____

Type of Room/Rate _____

Reservation Date/Deposit _____

Guest Name _____

Date/Time Arriving _____ Departing _____

Name of Hotel _____

Address/Phone _____

Type of Room/Rate _____

Reservation Date/Deposit _____

Guest Name _____

Date/Time Arriving _____ Departing _____

Name of Hotel _____

Address/Phone _____

Type of Room/Rate _____

Reservation Date/Deposit _____

Guest Name _____

Date/Time Arriving _____ Departing _____

Name of Hotel _____

Address/Phone _____

Type of Room/Rate _____

Reservation Date/Deposit _____

Guest Name _____

Date/Time Arriving _____ Departing _____

Name of Hotel _____

Address/Phone _____

Type of Room/Rate _____

Reservation Date/Deposit _____

WEDDING GUEST LIST

Name	Street, City, State, Zip	INVITED TO C - Ceremony R - Reception	RSVP Number Attending

WEDDING GUEST LIST

Name	Street, City, State, Zip	INVITED TO C - Ceremony R - Reception	RSVP Number Attending

WEDDING GUEST LIST

Name	Street, City, State, Zip	INVITED TO C - Ceremony R - Reception	RSVP Number Attending

ANNOUNCEMENT LIST

Name	Street, City, State, Zip	Gift	Thank you sent

WEEKEND WEDDING ITINERARY

Fill out, photocopy and send to each guest invited to the activities.

DAY _____   Date _____

    Activity _____ Time _____

    Location _____

    Dress _____

    Comment _____

DAY _____   Date _____

    Activity _____ Time _____

    Location _____

    Dress _____

    Comment _____

DAY _____   Date _____

    Activity _____ Time _____

    Location _____

    Dress _____

    Comment _____

DAY _____   Date _____

    Activity _____ Time _____

    Location _____

    Dress _____

    Comment _____

DAY _____   Date _____

    Activity _____ Time _____

    Location _____

    Dress _____

    Comment _____

Invitations and Stationery

GUEST LIST FOR WEEKEND ACTIVITIES

Day/Date	Time	Activity	Guest Attending

CHAPTER EIGHT

The Wedding Party

After giving some thought to the style of wedding you would like, you and your fiancé should determine the number of attendants, and who they will be. Before asking everyone you know, consider the size of the overall wedding, its location and your budget. Don't forget the more attendants, the more bouquets, boutonnieres, and gifts to buy.

When deciding who to ask, use some discretion. It can be difficult, and you don't want hurt feelings, but you just can't have everyone. Choose close friends and family members who are special to you, and for whom it won't be a financial burden.

Your attendants will not only give you moral support, but they add helpful hands, and will add a colorful backdrop to your wedding pictures.

MAID OR MATRON OF HONOR

Brides usually choose a maid or matron of honor they feel close to: a sister or best friend. If you're having a large wedding you may want both – a married sister for the matron, and an unmarried sister or friend for the maid of honor.

Your maid or matron of honor is indispensable and a big help throughout your planning and ceremony. Her customary duties include the following:

- Helps the bride with lots of details such as addressing envelopes, making favors and helping with the shopping.

- Pays for her own wedding attire.

- Alone, or with bridesmaids, has a shower for the bride. (This is optional.)

- Helps organize the bridesmaids with their fittings, and on the wedding day.

- Keeps the groom's ring until the appropriate time in the ceremony, when she exchanges it for the bride's bouquet.

- Assists the bride in dressing before the ceremony, and at the reception before the bride leaves.

- Signs the wedding certificate as a legal witness.

- Assists the bride with the train and veil at the altar.

- Is a member of the receiving line, and is seated in a place of honor at the reception.

BRIDESMAIDS

There are no definite rules on the number of bridesmaids you should have. However, twelve is customarily the limit and most do not have more than eight. For a simple wedding you should have fewer.

You may have an even or uneven number. With three or less, the bridesmaids walk single file down the aisle and precede the maid of honor. With an even number of four or more, you may want them to walk in pairs. If the bridesmaids outnumber the ushers in the recessional, the extras can pair up or walk alone. Most brides try to keep the same number of bridesmaids and ushers because it makes for symmetry at the altar and in the pictures. They are usually close friends or sisters of the bride or groom, and have few traditional duties, but add a colorful touch to the wedding.

The bridesmaids:

- May be helpful with the pre-wedding errands and tasks.

- Purchase their own wedding attire.

- May, alone or together, have a shower for the bride, and attend all pre-wedding parties.

- Attend the rehearsal and rehearsal dinner party.

- Sometimes participate in the receiving line.

THE BEST MAN

The groom usually chooses his brother, a close relative, or best friend; however, it can be the groom's father, or son, in the case of a second marriage. The best man not only offers moral support, but is the groom's right hand man in organizing activities and handling important duties.

- Pays for his own wedding attire.

- Transports the groom to the church and helps him dress.

- Supervises the ushers' fittings and organizes them on the wedding day.

- Keeps the bride's wedding ring until the appropriate time during the ceremony.

- Delivers the officiant's fee before or after the ceremony.

- Signs the wedding certificate as a witness.

- Makes the first toast to the bride and groom at the reception and reads any telegrams.

- Dances with the bride.

- Sees that the suitcases are loaded into the honeymoon car, and that the groom has his plane ticket, itinerary and traveler's checks.

- Takes the groom's wedding attire to the cleaners or to the rental shop.

THE USHERS OR GROOMSMEN

Like the bridesmaids, there is no definite number of ushers. A guide to follow is one usher for every 50 guests. Generally the size of the wedding determines the number. For example, you wouldn't want ten ushers with only fifty guests.

It is not necessary to have the same number of ushers as bridesmaids; however, it is better balanced if they are close in number. The ushers walk down the aisle in the processional singly, if less than four, and may be paired with four or more, if you like.

The ushers or groomsmen are usually brothers, relatives or close friends of the bride or groom. Their duties include the following:

- Pay for their wedding attire.

- Arrive at the church one hour before the ceremony to seat the early guests.

- Seat people with pew cards in the reserved or special section.

- Distribute wedding service programs if any.

- Seat the bride's guests, usually on the left and the groom's on the right. (In the Orthodox Jewish wedding the sides are reversed.)

- Direct the placement of wedding gifts.

- Seat the groom's parents in the right front pew and then the bride's mother in the left front row. She is the last person seated before the processional begins.

- They unroll the aisle carpet, then take their places.

- Escort the bridesmaids out of the church after the recessional.

THE FLOWER GIRL

You may have one or two little flower girls. They should be about the same size. Usually the range in age is from four to eight. Tiny tots, although very cute, are too young to understand what's going on and may be distracting.

She may carry a basket of rose petals that she scatters down the aisle, or a small bouquet. Or if rose petals are prohibited in your church, she may carry baby roses to pass out as she walks down the aisle.

RINGBEARER OR TRAINBEARER

It is not necessary to have either a ringbearer or trainbearer. However, if you do know one or two cute little boys about four or five, you may want to let them take part. The ringbearer or trainbearer may also be a little girl. If so, she should be dressed the same as the flower girl. The duties are minimal, but the children look adorable and add a special touch.

- The ringbearer carries the ring or rings tied by a ribbon on a satin or lacy pillow.

- The ringbearer may walk alone or with the flower girl, but precedes the bride.

- The trainbearer carries the bridal gown train, following the bride down the aisle.

MOTHER OF THE BRIDE

I'm sure she is as excited as you are and will want to be involved whenever it is possible, or when she is needed. Her involvement may depend on where she is located in relation to you or the wedding. However, even if there is a distance, she can help with advice and decisions. Her involvement may include:

- Assists with the selection of the gown, accessories, and attendants' attire.

- Compiles the guest list and helps address invitations.

- Assists in the ceremony and reception details.

- Purchases her own dress; she has the first choice in color but consults with the groom's mother.

- Keeps the father of the bride informed of wedding plans.

- Is official hostess at the wedding reception. She is the last person seated at the ceremony and the first to greet the guests in the receiving line. She is seated in a place of honor at the reception.

FATHER OF THE BRIDE

This is a big day for him, and one many proud fathers have waited for –escorting his beloved daughter down the aisle to give her away. Some brides prefer to walk alone. Although this is acceptable today, you may give it some thought before denying your father this pleasure.

- His wedding attire conforms to the groom's and other attendants'.

- He rides with the bride to the ceremony.

- He escorts his daughter down the aisle, and either stays there or sits in the front left pew.

- He may stand in the receiving line or mingle with guests as the host of the reception.

- He takes care of final payments of caterers, musicians, etc., and is generally the last person to leave the reception.

GROOM'S PARENTS

They may be as involved as you make them, depending on their financial involvement, and proximity to the wedding.

- Send a note or phone the bride and her parents welcoming her into their family.

- Generally host the rehearsal dinner party.

- Groom's mother stands in the receiving line, the father may or may not.

OTHER PARTICIPANTS

There are a number of honorary duties that may be assigned to other friends or relatives.

- Help decorate the ceremony or reception locations.

- Read a scripture or poem, or serve as candlelighters.

- Be in charge of the guest book and the gifts.

CHILDREN FROM PREVIOUS MARRIAGES

Children from previous marriages can be included to any degree you and your fiancé choose. Remember, this can be a difficult time for children. The more they are included and made to feel an important part of the wedding, the easier it will be for them to accept it. Depending on the ages of the children, there are a number of wonderful ways to include children. (See chapter on second marriages for ideas and information to include children.)

HANDLING DIVORCED PARENTS

In weddings involving divorced parents every situation must be handled somewhat differently, depending on the individual circumstances. If the parents have been divorced a long time, both are happily remarried, and they are friendly toward one another, you're lucky and there probably won't be any problems. Nevertheless, it is a good idea to involve all parents. Try to avoid favoritism that could result in hurt feelings.

If the two parents do not get along, sit down with both separately to remind them that this is your one special day and they should forget their differences and conceal their personal feelings.

Invitations

When it comes to sending invitations, and the bride's parents are divorced, there are a number of ways to word them. Examples are given in the chapter on *Invitations*. When the parents are separated but not legally divorced, it is best to ignore their differences and follow normal procedures for sending invitations.

Seating for the Ceremony

In a church, the mother of the bride should sit in the first pew on the left side. If she is remarried, her husband may sit with her. If she is not, she should sit alone or with close relatives. Any escort she may have should be seated with the other guests.

After giving his daughter away, the father may also sit in the first pew. Relatives can be seated between the two. This depends on the parents' feelings and should be discussed with both of them ahead of time. The father might also sit in the second or third row, especially if he is re-married and his wife is attending. In this case also, a casual escort should not sit in the front, but should be seated with the rest of the guests.

Receiving Line

A traditional receiving line begins with the bride's mother as hostess, and, if the fathers are included, they should stand to the left of their wives. With divorced parents, since it's not neces-sary to include fathers, it's probably best to leave both fathers out of the receiving line. They usually prefer to mingle among the guests anyway. How-ever, if they want to be part of the receiving line, they may stand next to their ex-wife, or be sepa-rated from her by the bride and groom, depending on the situation. Step parents are usu-ally left out of the receiving line, unless the bride or groom has no mother or father, or was raised by the step parent.

Remember, every family situation is different; ask your parents and step parents what makes them feel the most comfortable.

Seating at the Reception

At the reception, it is usually best not to in-clude divorced parents at the bride's table. Seat them at separate tables with members of their own family or friends. If the divorced parents are not on the best of terms, or if one is accompanied by his or her new spouse, consider placing the tables at opposite sides of the room.

BRIDE'S ATTENDANTS LIST

Maid of Honor _____ City _____ Phone _____

Address _____ Duties _____

Sizes _____

Bridesmaid _____

Address _____

City _____ Phone _____

Duties _____

Sizes _____

Bridesmaid _____

Address _____

City _____ Phone _____

Duties _____

Sizes _____

Bridesmaid _____

Address _____

City _____ Phone _____

Duties _____

Sizes _____

Bridesmaid _____

Address _____

City _____ Phone _____

Duties _____

Sizes _____

Bridesmaid _____

Address _____

City _____ Phone _____

Duties _____

Sizes _____

Bridesmaid _____

Address _____

City _____ Phone _____

Duties _____

Sizes _____

Bridesmaid _____

Address _____

City _____ Phone _____

Duties _____

Sizes _____

Bridesmaid _____

Address _____

City _____ Phone _____

Duties _____

Sizes _____

Junior Bridesmaid _____

Address _____

City _____ Phone _____

Duties _____

Sizes _____

Flower Girl _____

Address _____

City _____ Phone _____

Duties _____

Sizes _____

BRIDAL ATTENDANTS' INFORMATION

Photocopy and give a copy to each attendant.

FIRST FITTING (date/time) _____/_____   Final fitting (date/time) _____/_____

Location _____

- Make sure you have everything for the wedding day

    ❏ Dress   ❏ Shoes   ❏ Lingerie   ❏ Hosiery
    ❏ Gloves   ❏ Hat   ❏ Jewelry   ❏ Makeup

- Break in your shoes, if they are new.
- Have your hair washed and your nails done.
- Get plenty of rest the night before.

BRIDAL LUNCHEON

Date _____ Time _____ Phone _____

Location _____

Address _____

CEREMONY REHEARSAL

Date _____ Time _____ Phone _____

Location _____

Address _____

REHEARSAL DINNER

Date _____ Time _____ Phone _____

Location _____

Address _____

WEDDING DAY

Arrival time _____ Phone _____

Location _____

Where to dress _____

Photograph location _____ Time _____

TRANSPORTATION

To the ceremony _____

To the reception _____

OTHER

_____

_____

GROOM'S ATTENDANTS LIST

Best Man _____ City _____ Phone _____

Address _____ Duties _____

Sizes: _____

Usher _____ | **Usher** _____
Address _____ | Address _____
City _____ Phone _____ | City _____ Phone _____
Duties _____ | Duties _____
Sizes _____ | Sizes _____

Usher _____ | **Usher** _____
Address _____ | Address _____
City _____ Phone _____ | City _____ Phone _____
Duties _____ | Duties _____
Sizes _____ | Sizes _____

Usher _____ | **Usher** _____
Address _____ | Address _____
City _____ Phone _____ | City _____ Phone _____
Duties _____ | Duties _____
Sizes _____ | Sizes _____

Usher _____ | **Usher** _____
Address _____ | Address _____
City _____ Phone _____ | City _____ Phone _____
Duties _____ | Duties _____
Sizes _____ | Sizes _____

Ringbearer _____ | **Trainbearer or Page** _____
Address _____ | Address _____
City _____ Phone _____ | City _____ Phone _____
Duties _____ | Duties _____
Sizes _____ | Sizes _____

CHAPTER NINE

Bridal Gown and Accessories

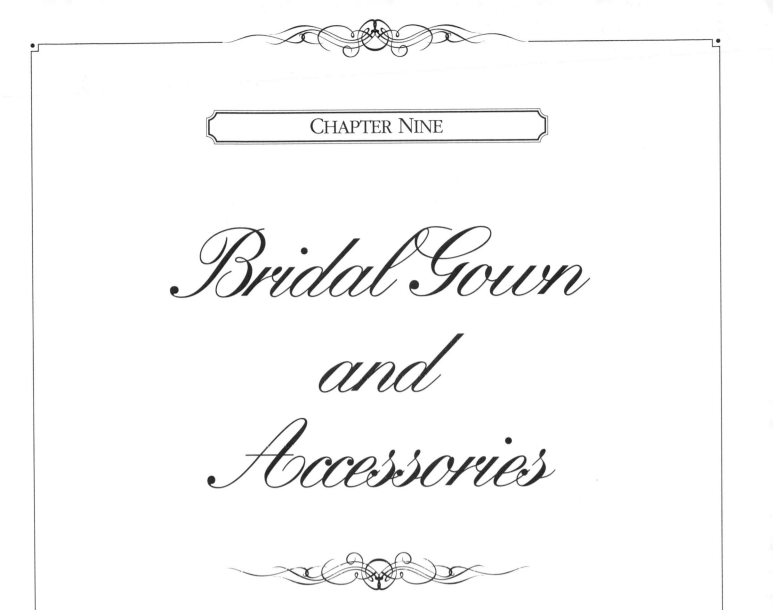

Every bride-to-be has fantasized about her wedding day, and what she will look like walking down the aisle. To approach those fantasies, try to determine the overall look you want for your wedding. Remember the bride sets the style. Harmony is the key to a beautiful wedding, no matter how formal and elaborate, or how simple.

There are many things to consider when determining what type of dress will be appropriate for your wedding. For example: the season will effect the types of fabric and colors used, there may be religious guidelines, or formality may determine the length of your gown, train, veil and the bridesmaids' dresses. The location also plays an important part in the feel or look of your wedding. If your ceremony is in a very modern or contemporary church, I would not advise trying to attain an old fashioned or Victorian look.

To determine your theme, you must start by deciding what is most important to you and plan the rest of the wedding around that. Have you always dreamed of a summer garden wedding with a blue sky and fresh flowers, or an elegant cathedral train worn for a High Noon Mass? Or is there a quaint old chapel you have always loved and thought of leaving in a horsedrawn carriage?

SELECTING YOUR GOWN

Once you have determined your theme, find the dress of your dreams. All brides look beautiful. Remember, the most important thing is that you feel beautiful. It's your Special Day so choose something that makes you feel that way.

- **Start Looking Early**. You will need to order your gown four to six months before your wedding, even earlier if you're having a bridal portrait done.

- **Determine Your Style**. Start by looking through the latest issues of bridal magazines, saving the pictures of the dresses you like best. Note the name of the manufacturer, or the bridal issue, on the picture. It makes for easier reference later. Find out from your church if there are any restrictions regarding off-the-shoulder or low-cut gowns. Next consider which style would look best on your figure type. (See section on choosing the best style for you.)

- **Set Your Budget**. Determine what you have to spend on your gown and accessories. Wedding gowns vary in price from a few hundred dollars to several thousand. Be realistic about what you can spend and don't forget about your headpiece, shoes, special full slip, etc. Your cost can rise very quickly, with the addition of these extras.

- **Find a Reputable Salon**. With your budget in mind, start looking in bridal salons. You may want to call ahead since some require appointments. If your schedule permits, try to shop on a week day. You will get better service, and won't feel rushed. (See section on How to Find a Reputable Salon.)

- **Bring Your Mother or a Friend**. It's always more fun to shop with your mother, sister, or best friend; you will want their opinion. However, don't confuse things by shopping with too many people. Ask a friend who has tastes similar to your own.

- **Bring Accessories**. When shopping for your gown, bring shoes similar to those you plan on wearing, and a strapless or backless bra, if you have one. The salon may or may not have bras, but will usually have a full slip to try on with the gown. If you're wearing a special necklace, earrings, or heirloom gloves, bring those with you.

- **Finding the Perfect Dress**. Bridal salons stock many, sometimes hundreds, of sample gowns, and finding the perfect one can be overwhelming. It's easiest if you enlist the assistance of a helpful sales consultant. She can narrow the selection down by showing you appropriate dresses once you tell her your budget, the date and type of wedding, and the style dress you prefer, or show her pictures of gowns you have selected from magazines.

ORDERING YOUR GOWN

When ordering a custom gown be absolutely certain of your decision. Most salons require a 50% deposit when the dress is ordered. Be sure to check exchange and cancellation policies. They differ from place to place. The gown is ordered to your nearest size then fitted to you perfectly. For your fitting make sure to take the shoes and undergarments you plan to wear on your wedding day.

Some bridal salons include one fitting in the cost of the gown, but most do not. Be sure to ask about the additional charges for any special alterations, including headpieces and veils. You don't want any last minute surprises. Get a contract or deposit receipt with the total amount and the date the dress will be ready.

Tips on Ordering a Gown

- Many designers have both a high end and a lower end line of gowns, usually under a different name, and using different quality fabric and lace.

- Some designers have their gowns made overseas. These gowns can be considerably less expensive because they are mass produced, rather than custom made when ordered.

- Be cautious! Don't order from hotel sales or people who ask for all the money up front, unless you leave with the gown; even then, inspect it. Even if the salesperson only requires a 50% deposit, be careful if he or she doesn't have a store. Brides have been known to make a deposit on a gown, then never again see the person who sold it to them.

CHOOSING THE BEST STYLE FOR YOU

Once you have determined the price and formality of the gown, you will want to find one to flatter your figure. Don't worry! There will be a perfect dress for you no matter what your size and shape.

These are some suggestions to help you find the perfect dress for your figure.

- **If You're Short** (under five feet four inches). A high neckline with an empire waist, a short sleeved or sleeveless dress, with long gloves, will make you look taller. The veil should not be longer than floor or chapel length.

- **If You're Tall** (over five feet nine inches). A drop waist with a wide belt and trim or ruffles that wraps around the dress will take away the all legs look. Off the shoulder, low necklines with billowy sleeves are also good. Hats or dramatic veiling are striking and will not overpower you.

- **If You're Average Height and Weight** (five five to five eight). You're lucky and can get away with almost anything you'd like. You may want to select something which makes you look either shorter or taller depending on the groom's height.

- **If You're Slender.** You're the one everyone envies. You can add a few pounds by selecting a heavier fabric such as velvet, satin or moire. Choose a blousier bodice with a gathered waist and narrow sleeves.

- **If You're Heavy.** You will want to aim for a slimmer effect with a high waistline or an A-line dress with vertical lines. Stay away from lacy ruffles, clingy fabrics and puffed sleeves.

- **If You're Large Busted.** A V-shape or high neckline with a keyhole yoke is usually most flattering. Avoid empire or cinched waists, they accentuate larger breasts.

- **If You Have Wide Hips.** This common problem can be disguised with a flared skirt or A-line dress. The wide bottom may be balanced by a broad collar, puffed sleeves or a hat.

THE COLOR AND FABRIC

The color of your dress does not have to be stark white. There are many beautiful shades of ivory that are also popular. The color of your dress should be what looks most flattering on you, so try a dress in each color. If you already have a headpiece, you should try to match the color. Ivory is usually chosen for an old fashioned or antique look. A light pastel is another option that is more popular for second weddings.

Fabrics usually change and are determined by the season.

Fall or Winter Weddings

Usually a heavier fabric is selected for this time of year, and may be any one of these: satins, rich taffetas, a moire, or even velvet or a heavy lace.

Spring or Summer Weddings

For this time of year a lighter fabric such as chiffon, light-weight satin, eyelet linen, dotted Swiss, or a light-weight lace may be used.

SELECTING THE RIGHT HEADPIECE

The headpiece is the finishing touch to your bridal ensemble. You will want to choose the perfect piece to flatter your face and your wedding gown.

- **Choose a headpiece to complement your gown**. Your headpiece should match your dress in color, and coordinate in style and decoration. An elaborately detailed gown calls for a more ornate headpiece, while a simpler or less formal dress calls for a less elaborate headpiece. Your veil length should coordinate with the length of your gown; the shorter the dress, the shorter the veil. Wear a chapel or cathedral length veil with a train, a ballet or fingertip with an ankle-length dress, and a blusher with a short dress.

- **Find a headpiece that will flatter your face**. Try various styles until you find the perfect look. If your face is round and full, you need to add height with a tiara, pill box or a pouf added to the back of a headpiece. When your face is long and narrow, you need to add width; consider a wide-brimmed hat.

- **Consider your hairstyle when selecting your headpiece**. The length and style of your hair will have some effect on the type of head-piece that looks best. If your hair is long and full, consider wearing it back or up and away from your face.

- **Make sure the headpiece fits properly**. You don't want a headpiece that's too tight and will be uncomfortable. Then again, you don't want one that's too loose. Try the headpiece on, wear it for a while, turn your head, bend over, and practice walking. Make sure you can move easily, that it feels comfortable and doesn't feel like it might slip off at any moment.

- **Wearing the headpiece at the reception**. If you're planning to wear your headpiece to the reception, consider having the salon make the veil removeable, with snaps or Velcro®, to provide easier movement. Or change to a smaller hairpiece, such as a bow, banana clip, or comb decorated with fresh or fabric flowers, pearls and ribbons. Make sure your hair style will work well with both headpieces, if you choose to wear something different for the reception.

HAIR STYLES AND MAKEUP

Many brides prefer to do their own hair and wear it naturally. Others like to have something special done. If you are having it done at a salon, make an appointment in advance and try the style with the headpiece at that time.

You may choose to do your own makeup or hire a professional makeup artist to do you or the entire wedding party. If you do your own makeup, apply enough so that you have color and don't look washed out. But do not overdo it. Ideally, your makeup should look natural. Some tips for better photographs:

- Use a foundation close to your natural skin color.

- Avoid shiny skin by applying powder lightly with a brush to neck and face.

Bridal Gown and Accessories

- Line your eyes with a brown pencil.

- Do not use frosted liner or eyeshadow.

- Use brown or black mascara.

- Apply a blush which complements your skin tone to your cheekbones and blend upward.

- Line your lips with a pencil, then apply a pastel lipstick with a touch of gloss on the lower lip.

WEDDING SHOES AND STOCKINGS

Your stockings should be a sheer beige, champagne, ivory or white, depending on the color of your shoes and wedding gown. There are wonderful bridal hose available—some with appliques or exquisite lace designs.

Don't forget this important touch, you wouldn't want to be embarrassed when it's time to take off the garter.

A pump style shoe is best in a silk or satin, and can be dyed to match your dress. For an added touch you may want to cover shoes with matching lace. Make sure they are comfortable and that the heel is not too high. Be prepared for hours of standing.

Some brides choose to wear ballet slippers, depending on their height and the groom's. They can be purchased at some bridal salons, dance stores, or through mail order. A special touch is to cover them with lace, baby pearls, or appliqued roses.

WEDDING GLOVES AND JEWELRY

Gloves are optional depending on the degree of formality and the style of your wedding gown. These are the types of gloves available.

- **Long Gloves**. These should be worn in a formal wedding when the sleeves on your dress are short.

- **Short Gloves**. These should be worn with a less formal gown or a three-quarter length sleeve.

Make sure the glove is open for the ring finger. Your engagement ring can be worn under the glove on the right hand and transferred after the ceremony.

Other Jewelry

If other jewelry is to be worn, it is best to keep it simple. You may want to wear a single pendant or strand of pearls if the neckline is open. You may wear pearl or diamond earrings. These add a nice touch if your ears show. Do not wear watches or heavy bracelets.

If you don't have this type of jewelry, it can be your something borrowed, rather than something you purchased.

WEDDING ACCESSORIES TO SHOP FOR

Garters

What about a pretty lacy garter? This could be your something blue. There are some beautiful, hand-detailed garters available, so pretty you will hate to toss it away. Buy one to keep and one to toss.

Hankies or Bibles

A nice touch of sentiment may be to carry an antique lace hanky or a family prayer book. This is something old. It could be something your mother carried down the aisle.

Guest Book

Don't forget, when shopping, to get a guest book – fun to look through in years to come. You may want to gather the same friends for a reaffirmation or 25th wedding anniversary. There is a wide variety of styles and colors in guest books. You may want to add your own touches of lace, or accent one with ribbon in your wedding color. Some specialty shops personalize guest books by embroidering your monogram on the front in your wedding color. If you're handy, make your own. Pick a solid color fabric, have the monogram, embroidered in a wedding color, placed in the center or at one corner, then trim with the same color ribbon. No one will have a guest book like yours!

Goblets

It's nice to have special goblets or personalized toasting glasses. They are something you'll have for years, and maybe want to use on each anniversary to celebrate. There is a variety of styles and prices, from expensive silver goblets to less expensive toasting glasses. You will surely find something you like within your budget.

Ring Pillow

If you are having a ringbearer, you will want to find just the right pillow for him or her to carry. That shouldn't be a problem; they can be found at many bridal salons or specialty shops that make pillows; or can be purchased through mail order companies. There are a number of styles, colors and shapes to choose from: round, square, rectangular, or heart-shaped, all equally beautiful. If you're talented, you may want to make your own and personalize it with your names or the date of the wedding.

PRESERVING THE GOWN

After the wedding, have your mother or maid of honor take the dress to a reliable cleaner. They will clean it. If you like, have it wrapped and sealed in a special airtight box. This will preserve your gown for possible future use by a friend or family member, or perhaps for you to wear again in a reaffirmation ceremony.

If you choose to preserve the gown yourself, here are some helpful hints. Never leave it on a hanger, or store it in a plastic bag. Fold the dress with layers of acid-free tissue (ask your cleaner where to purchase it). Then wrap it with unbleached muslin, which allows it to breathe. Store the gown in a cedar chest or a lined wooden drawer. Air it out yearly and fold it in different places before restoring. Make sure it is stored in a dark, dry place.

MONEY SAVINGS TIPS

- **Consider wearing a bridesmaid's dress in white for an informal wedding.**

- **Order bridesmaids' dresses from ready -to-wear designers**. There may be little or no savings, but your bridesmaids will have a dress they are more liable to wear again.

- **Rent a gown.** Over the last few years apparel rental stores have opened up in some major cities. Many stores rent both dressy formalwear and bridal gowns; others just specialize in bridal attire. Check the yellow pages in your area or in a large city nearby.

- **Hire a professional seamstress**. Having a seamstress design an original gown for you, or copy an existing design, can save you money when you are considering the purchase of an expensive gown. Remember, a lot of fabric, lace and labor go into making a wedding gown. The one area you will save on is alterations, so consider this in your comparison.

- **Sew your own gown**. If you, your mother or a friend have the time and a knack for sewing, this is a viable way to save money. Most large fabric stores have a section featuring bridal fabric, lace and patterns. Be sure you can handle the job; wedding gown fabrics can be slippery, especially when dealing with the lengths required for bridal gowns. You don't want to find yourself wasting a few hundred dollars on fabric, and then end up having to order a gown anyway.

- **Consignment shops or newspapers**. Sometimes you can find new or used gowns through either of these sources. Sometimes weddings are canceled, or newly-married brides are looking to recoup some of the money they just spent. The gown may need alterations and cleaning, so figure that into the cost and be sure to inspect the dress carefully. Start looking months in advance; you need to allow yourself plenty of time to order a gown if you don't find one using these sources.

- **Buy a gown from a canceled wedding**. Check with bridal salons in your area to see if they have gowns that have never been picked up. Sometimes a bride will put a deposit on a gown, the wedding is canceled, and she never returns to pick it up. The salon may be willing to sell the gown for the 50% balance that is still owing, since they have already collected a 50% deposit from the first bride.

- **Wear your mother's, sister's or a friend's gown**. Wearing a family heirloom gown can not only be cost saving, but can add a touch of sentiment to the ceremony. Borrowing a friend's or relative's gown can be a great way to save money.

- **Buy from a designer outlet store**. Some department stores or major designers send damaged, discontinued or overstocked merchandise to outlet stores in various parts of the country. Call department stores or designers to see if they have outlets, and where they are. A word of caution: Check merchandise carefully, and call the outlet to see if the store has what you are looking for before making a long trip.

- **Ask about package discounts**. Some salons may offer a discount on your gown if you purchase all the bridesmaids' dresses from them. This is often negotiable; it never hurts to ask!

- **Add your own touch**. Buy a simple, inexpensive gown from a salon, bead your own lace appliques, and add them to the gown, in order to give it a more elaborate look. Check local fabric stores for prices and availability of lace before going this route.

- **Save on shoes**. Buy shoes that can be dyed another color and can be worn again, or borrow shoes from a friend.

- **Order the gown in a less expensive fabric**. If the dress style you like is out of your price range, see if the dress can be made in a less expensive fabric.

- **Avoid expensive design changes**. Find a gown that has the design elements you want, and avoid expensive changes such as changing the train length or style of sleeve.

- **Minimize alterations**. Keep alterations to a minimum; order the closest size, to your largest measurement, from the manufacturer's size chart (each manufacturer's size chart varies).

BRIDAL ATTIRE SHOPPING WORKSHEET

Option # _____ Item _____ Store _____

Description _____

Manufacturer _____ Style # _____

Color _____ Size _____ Cost _____

Sales Contact _____ Phone _____

Option # _____ Item _____ Store _____

Description _____

Manufacturer _____ Style # _____

Color _____ Size _____ Cost _____

Sales Contact _____ Phone _____

Option # _____ Item _____ Store _____

Description _____

Manufacturer _____ Style # _____

Color _____ Size _____ Cost _____

Sales Contact _____ Phone _____

Option # _____ Item _____ Store _____

Description _____

Manufacturer _____ Style # _____

Color _____ Size _____ Cost _____

Sales Contact _____ Phone _____

Option # _____ Item _____ Store _____

Description _____

Manufacturer _____ Style # _____

Color _____ Size _____ Cost _____

Sales Contact _____ Phone _____

Option # _____ Item _____ Store _____

Description _____

Manufacturer _____ Style # _____

Color _____ Size _____ Cost _____

Sales Contact _____ Phone _____

Bridal Gown and Accessories

BRIDAL ATTIRE INFORMATION

BRIDAL SALON _____ Phone _____

Address _____

Salesperson _____ Date ordered _____

Payment Terms _____ Date Required _____

	Description	Cost	Deposit	Balance Due
Wedding Gown	_____			
Manufacturer	_____			
Style #	_____	_____	_____	_____
Headpiece	_____			
Manufacturer	_____			
Style #	_____	_____	_____	_____
Veil	_____			
Manufacturer	_____			
Style #	_____	_____	_____	_____

ACCESSORIES

Slip _____ _____ ❏ *(Picked up)*

Bra _____ _____ ❏ *(Picked up)*

Hosiery _____ _____ ❏ *(Picked up)*

Shoes _____ _____ ❏ *(Picked up)*

Garter _____ _____ ❏ *(Picked up)*

Gloves _____ _____ ❏ *(Picked up)*

Jewelry _____ _____ ❏ *(Picked up)*

Hair Accessories _____ _____ ❏ *(Picked up)*

Other _____ _____ ❏ *(Picked up)*

Total Cost _____

ALTERATIONS

Fitting dates/times:_____/_____   _____/_____ Final _____/_____

Alteration Person _____ Phone _____

Location _____ Cost _____

DELIVERY

Date _____ Time _____ ❏ Home ❏ Church ❏ Pick-up

PRESSING INSTRUCTIONS

_____

_____

BRIDAL ATTIRE WORKSHEET

	ESTIMATE #1		ESTIMATE #2	
	Name _____		Name _____	
	Phone _____		Phone _____	
	Description	**Cost**	**Description**	**Cost**
BRIDAL GOWN Designer Size Color/Fabric Train Length				
HEADDRESS/VEIL Style Color Veil Length				
UNDERGARMENTS Bra Slip Stockings				
SHOES Size Style Color Dyeing Charge				
ACCESSORIES Gloves Garter Hankie				
FITTINGS/ALTERATIONS				
TOTAL				

BRIDAL SALON CHOICE

Name _____

Address _____

Phone/Salesperson _____

Total Cost _____

Order Date/Deposit _____

Fitting Date _____

Pickup Date _____

Balance Due _____

CHAPTER TEN

The Wedding Party Attire

It is the bride's privilege to select the type of fabric and color of the attendants' dresses. It should be something that complements your gown and the overall look of the wedding. However, you will want the attendants to feel comfortable and attractive, too, so ask their opinions once you have narrowed the choice down to a few dresses that you like.

Bridesmaids' dresses are usually ordered through a bridal salon or made by the bridesmaids or a dressmaker. For a less traditional look, check the formal dress section of a better department store in your area. You may find something your attendants can wear in the future.

It is not a definite rule that the bridesmaids wear identical dresses, but it is best to keep them similar in style and color. Generally the bridesmaids are dressed alike; the maid or matron may be dressed the same or differently. If she is dressed the same, and in the identical color, give her a larger bouquet to set her apart from the others.

When selecting bridesmaids' dresses consider how they will look on each bridesmaid – and not only the style and color. Try to keep the cost within reason, or consider paying a portion of the cost as a bridesmaids' gift.

Bridesmaids' Shoes

If the bridesmaids' shoes are being dyed to match the dress, it is best they all be done in the same shop to ensure an exact match. Another option is to have the bridesmaids wear white, ivory, gold or silver shoes.

The Flower Girl

The flower girl's dress may match the bridesmaids' in color and may be short or floor length. Some wedding dresses have flower girl dresses that match. Or a short lacy party dress may be worn. Ballet slippers are often worn, in either white or pastel. A nice touch is to add lace and baby pearls around the opening of the slipper. Flower girls always look darling, especially carrying a basket of rose petals which has been decorated with ribbons. Add a flowered wreath woven with colored ribbons to her hair—she'll look just like a little angel.

THE MOTHERS

The dresses of the bride's and groom's mothers should be in harmony and within the overall look of the wedding in regard to style and color.

It is important that the dresses complement each other for the pictures. They should confer with you and each other on the length to be worn and whether or not to wear a hat or gloves.

MEN'S FORMAL WEAR

In most weddings the groom, best man, ushers, and even fathers rent their formal wear. A wide selection is available so it is best to look in a few shops before making a final decision. If possible, rent everything from the same shop, and if

not, at least get the same type of suit. There are many choices available. Select something to fit your formality and the season, and one which will blend nicely with the other colors.

Consider having the groom's father in the same outfit as the others. This looks better for pictures and in the receiving line. The bride's father should always be dressed in accordance with the groom and the attendants.

MEN'S SEMI-FORMAL WEAR

For a great look at that less formal wedding, put the groom and attendants in suits and ties. For evening or winter, generally navy, black or dark grey is worn. A light white, or ivory, suit is worn for summer afternoons. If the groom's suit is white or ivory, it should match the bride's dress. If she wears ivory, then he should not wear stark white.

With many wonderful things to select from, remember to keep the overall look in mind. Pastel shirts and jackets are not as popular as they once were. However, if chosen, make sure the color blends with the bridesmaids' dresses. This goes without saying: dark shoes and socks with dark suits and light shoes and socks with light ones.

RINGBEARER OR TRAINBEARER

Usually the ringbearer and trainbearer are little boys. If this is the case, dress them the same as, or similar to, the groom or his attendants. If not identical, then keep in the same color scheme. Depending on the formality, and the size of the boy, he can wear a tuxedo, light or dark suit, or perhaps knickers with knee socks for a less formal garden wedding.

GUIDE TO DAYTIME WEDDING ATTIRE

Wedding Style	Bride	Bridesmaids	Groom & Attendants	Mothers
VERY FORMAL *200 guests or more, noon, afternoon*	Same as very formal evening, but short train is also appropriate.	Four to 12, Same over-all style as very formal evening, but dresses are often less elaborate.	Traditional: Cutaway coat, gray striped trousers, gray waistcoat, wing-collared shirt, ascot or striped tie. (Optional: Top hat, spats, gray glove.) Contemporary: Contoured long or short jacket, wing collared shirt.	Floor-length dresses no so formal as those for evening. Same accessories as those worn for evening.
FORMAL DAYTIME *100 guests*	Same as formal evening, but an elaborate, short dress worn with a bridal headpiece with short veil is also acceptable.	Two to six. Dresses either long or street length, but not too elaborate. Matching or harmonizing accessories, including bouquet.	Traditional: Gray stroller, waistcoat, striped trousers, shirt, striped tie. (Optional: Homburg, gloves.) Contemporary: Groom may choose formal suit in white or light colors for summer, darker shades for fall, dress shirt, bow tie, vest or cummerbund. Groomsmen coordinate with similar ensembles.	Elegant dress or suit usually street length. Flowers to wear, other accessories to match or harmonize.
SEMI-FORMAL DAYTIME *100 guests or fewer, often home.*	Street-length dress, white or pastel color, short veil. Small bouquet or flower-trimmed prayer book.	Seldom more than one. Same as semi-formal evening, but dresses are simpler.	Traditional: Favorite suit, white, colored or striped shirt, four-in-hand tie. Contemporary: Dinner jacket or formal suit, dress shirt, bow tie, vest or cummerbund.	Same as semi-formal evening dress, but less elaborate.
INFORMAL *family, daytime*	Suit or street dress. Hat, gloves, shoes and bag. Nosegay or flowers to wear.	Maid of honor only. Dress or suit similar to bride's. Flowers to wear.	Same as semi-formal.	Dresses or suits, similar to honor attendant's.

GUIDE TO EVENING WEDDING ATTIRE

Wedding Style	Bride	Bridesmaids	Groom & Attendants	Mothers
VERY FORMAL EVENING *200 guests or more after 6 p.m.*	Dress with a long train. Veil to complement dress, often long or full. Long sleeves or gloves to cover arms. Shoe to match dress. Full bouquet or flower-trimmed prayer book.	Four to 12. Long dresses, short veils, or other headpieces, gloves to complement sleeve length. Any style bouquet, shoes to match or harmonize.	Traditional: Full dress tailcoat with matching trousers, white waistcoat, white bow tie, wing collared shirt. (Optional: Black top hat, white gloves.) Contemporary: Black contoured long or short jacket, wing collared shirt.	Floor length evening dinner dresses. Small hats. Shoes, gloves and flowers harmonize.
FORMAL EVENING *100 guests or more, after 6 pm*	Long dress with a chapel or sweep train. Veil of a length to complement dress. Accessories the same as those for very formal wedding.	Two to six. Similar to very formal, but dresses are sometimes short. Gloves are optional.	Traditional: Dark dinner jacket with matching trousers, dress shirt, bow tie, vest or cummerbund. (Optional: White or ivory jackets in summery climate.) Contemporary look would be the same as formal daytime. Groomsmen coordinate with similar ensembles.	Dinner dresses, usually long. Small hats, shoes, gloves and flowers harmonizing with dress.
SEMI-FORMAL EVENING *100 guests or fewer, home chapel*	Trainless, floorlength or shorter dress white or pastel. Veil, elbow length or shorter. Same accessories as for a formal wedding, but simpler bouquet is used.	Seldom more than one, plus an honor attendant. Elaborate, street length dresses. Small bouquets.	Traditional: Favorite suit, white, colored or striped shirt, four-in-hand tie. Contemporary: Dinner jacket of formal suit, dress shirt, bow tie, vest or cummerbund.	Elaborate street length dresses with appropriate accessories.
INFORMAL *family, evening*	Suit or street dress. Hat gloves, shoes and bag. Nosegay or flowers to wear.	Maid of honor only. Dress or suit similar to wear	Same as semi-formal.	Dresses or suits similar to honor attendants.

BRIDE'S ATTENDANTS WORKSHEET

	ESTIMATE #1 Salon Name _____ Phone _____		**ESTIMATE #2** Salon Name _____ Phone _____	
	Description	**Cost**	**Description**	**Cost**

MAID/MATRON OF HONOR DRESS
    Color/Fabric
    Size
    Manufacturer
    Style #				

BRIDESMAIDS' DRESSES
    Color/Fabric
    Sizes
    Manufacturer
    Style #				

FLOWERGIRL'S DRESS
    Color/ Fabric
    Size
    Manufacturer
    Style #				

SHOES/STOCKINGS
    Style
    Sizes
    Dyeing Charge				

ACCESSORIES
    Hat
    Gloves
    Other				

FITTINGS/ALTERATIONS				
TOTAL				

BRIDAL SALON CHOICE

Name _____   Order Date/Deposit _____

Address _____   Fitting Date _____

Phone/Salesperson _____   Pickup Date _____

Cost of each outfit _____   Balance Due _____

GROOM'S ATTENDANTS WORKSHEET

	ESTIMATE #1		**ESTIMATE #2**	
	Name _____		Name _____	
	Phone _____		Phone _____	
	Description	**Cost**	**Description**	**Cost**
GROOM Style Color Size				
ATTENDANTS Style Color Size				
RING/TRAINBEARER Style Color Size				
FATHERS Style Color Sizes				
SHOES				
ACCESSORIES Hat Gloves Other				
TOTAL				

FORMALWEAR SHOP CHOICE

Name _____

Address _____

Phone/Salesperson _____

Fitting Date _____

Pickup Date _____ Return Date _____

Deposit _____ Balance Due _____

Groom _____

Each Attendant _____

Child Attendant _____

Each Father _____

ATTENDANTS' SIZES AND MEASUREMENTS

BRIDAL ATTENDANTS' SIZES AND MEASUREMENTS

Attendant's Name	Dress	Shoe	Hose	Slip	Glove	Head

GROOM'S ATTENDANTS' MEASUREMENTS

Attendant's Name	Coat	Sleeve	Neck	Waist	Inseam	Shoe

CHAPTER ELEVEN

Planning the Reception

There are a number of things to consider when planning your reception. Whether it is to be large or small, formal or informal, it is always best to have your reception immediately following the ceremony and to select a style that complements your wedding theme. Other things to consider, besides your personal preference, are the number of guests you invite and your budget.

SELECTING THE LOCATION

The location you select will be determined by your choice, the availability on your date, the number of people to be accommodated and the price. Make sure to find out exactly what is, or is not, included in the price. Unexpected extras can add up quickly. Do not delay in reserving the location once you have made your decision; popular places are reserved early. The following are some things to keep in mind when selecting a location.

Churches or Temples

• Check to see what type of hall or social room they have and what their fee is.

• If you plan to serve alcoholic beverages or wine, be sure to inquire about the policies.

• Find out what accessories they provide such as: tables, chairs, linens, china and silver.

• Check on any music restrictions they might have.

• Be sure you may have a caterer of your choice.

Private Clubs, Hotels, or Restaurants

• These locations are probably the easiest to consider. They offer complete service and facilities and they will coordinate all phases of your reception.

• Make sure you see the actual room or location where the reception would take place.

• Discuss the menu selections and the costs per person of each. Does it include the cake ?

• Make sure to check liquor and beverage fees. What is the charge per drink for an open bar? Is there a corking fee if you provide your own champagne? Do they charge extra to pour coffee with the cake?

• Find out what equipment is included, what will be extra, and what will be rented – dance floor, microphone, etc.

• Check on music restrictions.

• Know exactly how long you may have the facilities.

• Make sure they have adequate serving people. Most commercial places add a service fee. Be sure to find out what that will be.

• See if decorations and flowers are handled separately or if they are provided.

The advantage with these locations is that the people are experienced, and relieve you of the burdens of coordinating the reception.

The disadvantages are that you must conform to their time schedule, and many times, to pre-established menus which allow little or no flexibility.

Home or Garden

Private homes and gardens can offer more flexibility with regard to personal desires and time schedules. However, the burden of coordinating is on you and may require the assistance of a wedding coordinator.

• Make sure the location can accommodate all your guests.

• Depending on the type of reception, the food can be prepared by you with the help of family and friends. I don't advise this unless for budget reasons you have no choice. This is one party you, your family and friends should enjoy. You will have enough to worry about.

• Discuss your desires with a few caterers to determine what costs are involved. (This is discussed in more detail later in the chapter.)

• Make a detailed list of all the equipment that will need to be rented, and determine the costs. (This list is covered under caterers.)

• Arrange parking. Is it adequate, or will you need valet service?

• Check the kitchen and bathroom facilities. Are they adequate or will portable stoves and toilets need to be supplied?

• Survey the lighting that is available. Is there sufficient electricity for outside lights or heaters?

• If planning a garden reception, make sure it can be moved inside, the area can be tented, or you have an alternative location in the event of bad weather.

Planning the Reception

- Send a note letting your neighbors know that a wedding reception will be taking place, especially for an evening reception with a band. This may prevent any problems that might otherwise occur.

Reception Location Ideas:

- Church or Synagogue halls
- Private club facilities
- Community centers
- Elks or Women's Club facilities
- Condominium or private estate clubhouse facilities
- Museums
- Art galleries
- Historical buildings or mansions
- Public beaches and parks
- Public gardens
- Zoos or amusement parks
- Movie studio lots
- Private homes and estates for rent
- Wineries, ranches or orchards
- Fairgrounds
- Racetracks
- Banks or larger lobbies of grand old buildings
- Civic or private theaters
- Bed and breakfast inns
- Romantic restaurants
- Hotel ballrooms
- Yachts, boats or barges
- University facilities
- Military club facilities
- A romantic resort
- Your home or a friend's home
- Any place beautiful, interesting or romantic in your area

TYPES OF RECEPTIONS

If you have determined the time and style of your wedding, and considered the number of guests and size of your budget, you probably have a good idea of the type of reception that will suit your needs and desires. Listed below are the various types of receptions.

Morning

A breakfast or brunch reception is nice following a morning wedding at 9 or 10 o'clock. This may be served buffet style, or the guests may be seated at specified tables.

If you choose buffet style, an assortment of fresh fruit, croissants, rolls and quiches, with a variety of cold cuts and cheeses are nice. Hot coffee, tea and fresh juice should be served.

With a sit-down breakfast you may want to start with fresh juice and fruit, then serve an omelette or Eggs Benedict with toast or rolls for the entree. Hot coffee and tea are a must.

Pastries or a wedding cake should be served. Serving alcoholic beverages is optional but may include champagne, champagne punch, wine, screwdrivers or bloody Marys.

Luncheon

These are similar to brunch receptions and may be either sit-down or buffet style. They generally follow a late morning or high noon ceremony and are served between 12 and 2 pm.

Buffet luncheons may include a variety of salads, such as; potato, fruit, chicken, pasta or vegetables with dip. Poached salmon and shrimp are popular, but also expensive. Sandwiches, cold cuts, and cheeses are often served, and are relatively inexpensive. Your reception coordinator or caterer will have suggestions, according to your budget.

Sit-down luncheons may be started by serving champagne, cocktails, and hors d'oeuvres while guests go through the receiving line. Once the guests are seated, a white wine may be served with soup or salad to start. Then boned breast of chicken, a chicken crepe or beef entree with rice and vegetables is nice.

Serve coffee or tea with the wedding cake. Having an espresso/cappuccino bar, or offering chocolate cups filled with cordials adds a nice touch.

Tea or Cocktail

Tea receptions are generally held between 2:00 and 5:00, usually starting not later than 3:30.

Coffee, tea or punch, both with and without champagne or wine, are generally served. Tea sandwiches or other finger food, along with wedding cake, is the basic requirement.

This type of reception is the least expensive to have, and perfect when there is a large guest list and a small budget. If held in a home or garden, this type of reception will cut down on rentals.

Cocktail receptions are held between 4:00 and 7:30 pm. If only cocktails are being served, with no dinner to follow, the reception should start by 5:30 or 6:00 at the latest.

Usually champagne, wine, punch, or beer are served and in many cases there is an open bar, depending on the budget. Hot and cold hors d'oeuvres may be passed or set out on buffet tables.

Dinner

A dinner reception is usually started sometime between 6:00 and 9:00 pm. In many cases cocktails and hors d'oeuvres are served in the first hour, with a sit-down or buffet dinner following.

Such cocktail service will add to your expenses. (To keep expenses down, offer wine and beer, rather than a full bar.) A cocktail hour of some kind gives people time to go through the receiving line and mingle with friends, especially when a sit-down dinner follows.

Sit-Down Receptions

As mentioned before, and quite obviously, this is a party where the guests are served at the table. It usually, but not always, has a more formal feeling, and most of the time is preceded by a cocktail hour so the guests can mingle. A sit-down reception provides for more organization. It is easier to get the guests' attention when the traditional ceremonies, such as cutting the cake, are to begin. On the other hand some people feel the sit-down service tends to quiet a party down, and discourages people from mingling.

Buffet Receptions

A buffet reception is one in which the guests serve themselves. They may choose to sit at a table of their choice, or seats may be assigned. The buffet table is arranged with a variety of food, and can be either round or oblong, with the food placed around the edge. It may also be rectangular with food served from behind one side, or with food displayed along both sides. The way the tables are arranged will be determined by the area available and the number of guests. Try to avoid making the guests wait in a long line. For a larger number of guests have two buffet tables, one at each end of the room.

Food Station Receptions

Another idea which is unique and adds to the decor of the area, is what is called food stations. They are smaller buffet tables which are set up around the room, or in different areas of a garden. It is especially nice when each food station has a different theme and type of food. Decorate them with floral displays and unique serving pieces. They will not only look beautiful, but are a fun way for the guests to eat, and will increase the mingling of the guests. Try: a beautiful display of cheeses with breads and fresh fruits displayed in baskets, or an ice-carved boat filled with jumbo shrimp and crab legs. Or you may add to this eating adventure a chef carving a roast, serving hot won tons from a wok, or a chicken crepe made right in front of the guests' eyes.

RECEPTION TIPS

- Private clubs, restaurants or hotels which provide complete service and facilities many times can be less expensive, and relieve you of the burdens of coordinating the reception.

- Make sure you see the actual room or location where the reception will take place. Have the room name, or description, written on your contract to avoid any confusion later.

- Disadvantages with private clubs, restaurants or hotels are that you must conform to their time schedule, and, many times, to pre-established menus which allow little or no flexibility.

- Private homes or gardens can offer more flexibility with regard to personal desires and time schedules. However, the burden of coordinating is on you, and may require the assistance of a wedding coordinator.

- Interview a few caterers and reception location managers; compare the cost and what each will provide before making your final decision.

- When comparing cost of different locations, don't forget to add in the cost of rental equipment, such as tables, chairs, glasses, plates, silver and serving dishes, if you are considering a location that doesn't provide these items.

SPECIAL TOUCHES

- Add some fun to the reception; place plastic bottles of bubble-blowing liquid on tables, at each guest's place. Personalize the labels with the bride and groom's name and wedding date. Bubbles can fill the air as the bride and groom have their first dance. Or replace the tradition of throwing rice with bubbles, to wish the newlyweds well as they depart for their honeymoon.

- Use a small picture frame to double as a table or place card, and wedding favor all in one. Write each guest's name in calligraphy on a small piece of paper, slide it into the frame and place these frames appropriately at each table, or add the table number and hand them to guests as they enter the reception room. This doubles as a wedding favor that every guest can take home and enjoy.

- Place a throw-away camera on each table. Instruct the guests to take pictures during the reception. It will not only be entertaining, but you'll get a lot of great candid shots. Don't forget to arrange for someone to collect all the cameras at the end of the reception.

- Have each guest share a favorite memory they have of you or the groom. On the back of your wedding invitation, or on a separate enclosure, have your printer add your request that each guest share a favorite memory of the bride or groom. Instruct guests to write this memory on a piece of paper, sign it and bring it to the reception, where the papers will be collected and later put in a Memory Book. When planning a smaller, more intimate reception, consider having guests who wish to do so, read this memory aloud so everyone can share it. This adds fun and emotionally-touching moments that you and your guests will enjoy and remember.

MONEY SAVING TIPS

- **Get liquor wholesale**. Buy liquor from a wholesaler who will let you return unopened bottles.

- **Keep beverage cost down**. Serve a punch, wine only, or non-alcoholic drinks, like sparkling cider or grape juice.

- **Handle rentals yourself**. Get rentals directly from a rental company rather than through your caterer. You can avoid the middle man.

- **Decide on a morning or an afternoon reception**. A breakfast or brunch is less expensive than a dinner. For an afternoon reception, serve cake and hors d'oeuvres, rather than a full meal. Also, people tend to drink less earlier in the day.

- **Limit cocktail hour**. To save money, if having an open bar, limit the cocktail hour, and then serve only wine after that allotted time. Consider having someone pass drinks on a tray—this can help avoid people setting drinks down, then going to the bar to order another one.

- **Avoid selecting the most expensive menu items**. Items such as shrimp, lobster, crab and beef are more expensive than chicken or pasta.

- **Serve less expensive hors d'oeuvres**. Avoid serving hors d'oeuvres that are labor intensive or use expensive ingredients.

- **Serve food**. Have buffet food served by the caterer's staff, rather than have guests pile food, much of which will remain uneaten, on their plates themselves. This will also help avoid the embarrassment of running out of food – the nightmare of every hostess.

- **Cut guests list**. Reduce the size of your guest list, consider eliminating dates and children of friends, business associates and casual acquaintances.

- **Check hotel reception packages**. Some hotels have special reception packages, which include a discount on a bridal suite when the reception is held there, or when you book a block of rooms for out-of-town guests.

- **Home Wedding**. Have your reception in your or a friend's home or garden.

- **Use Disposable Plates**. Using paper plates, along with plastic cups and utensils, may be less expensive than renting china, glasses and silverware. Check rental prices in your area; don't forget to allow for breakage.

LIQUOR AND BEVERAGES

Since liquor, champagne, and other beverages are important parts of your reception, definite consideration should be given to what you would like and can afford. Prices will vary depending on the amount and the brand of alcohol served. It is an expected tradition that at least champagne or punch (for non-alcoholic receptions) be served to toast the couple. There are a number of serving options and variations, ranging from wine and beer only to an open bar with after dinner drinks.

Hotels, Restaurants and Clubs

If your reception is in a hotel, restaurant or club, check the type of alcohol the place supplies and the cost per drink. You may arrange to have an unlimited open bar for the entire time or limit it to a "cocktail hour," then serve wine with dinner, and coffee or after dinner drinks. If the hotel or restaurant allows you to provide your own wine or champagne, generally a separate "corkage fee" is charged per bottle. Be sure to check on this fee. Some places also charge extra to pour coffee. For smaller budgets you may only want to serve a champagne punch or a moderately priced wine with dinner.

When reviewing your alternatives, take into consideration that most people drink more in the evening and during warm weather. The average person consumes four to five drinks an evening, or approximately one every hour.

Providing Your Own Beverages

Your caterer may provide the alcohol, or may refer you to a reputable liquor dealer. Most liquor dealers can provide any brand you request, along with appropriate mixes. Dealers who provide this service arc well worth using. Most will deliver, and bring more than is usually consumed, so you won't run short. You are only charged for the bottles that are opened. Make sure to take an inventory of what was delivered, have someone keep an eye on the bartenders, and count both the opened and unopened bottles to make sure none have disappeared. Liquor dealers can also provide wine, beer and champagne. Their prices are considerably less than buying through a retail liquor store. They are experienced and can provide advice as to brands and quantities within your budget.

Be sure to provide non-alcoholic beverages, soft drinks or punch. Champagne punch or non-alcoholic punch can be prepared by the caterer, unless you arc doing the reception yourself.

PUNCH RECIPES

Champagne Punch

1 gal. Sauterne wine
4 quarts champagne
2 quarts ginger ale
1/2 pt. sherbert

Chill wine, champagne and ginger ale. Pour into large punch bowl, add sherbert, ice cubes or ice ring just before serving.

Non-Alcoholic Punch

2-12 oz. cans frozen orange juice
2-12 oz. cans frozen lemonade
8 cans of cold water
2 cups Grenadine
Juice of three fresh lemons
3 qts. ginger ale chilled

Mix together in large punch bowl just before serving, float orange slices and cherries on the top. Add ice cubes or ice ring.

Party Punch

1 fifth bourbon
8 oz. unsweetened pineapple juice
8 oz. unsweetened grapefruit juice
4 oz. fresh lemon juice
2 bottles (qt.) 7-Up

Pre-chill all the ingredients. Mix together just before serving, adding 7-Up last. Decorate with fruit and ice ring.

Hospitality Punch

1/2 gal. orange juice
1/2 gal. pineapple juice
1/2 gal. lime juice
2 quarts ginger ale
2 quarts light or dark rum
1/2 lb. sugar

Pre-chill all ingredients. Mix together just before serving, adding ginger ale last. Garnish with fresh fruit. Add ice cubes or ice ring.

QUESTIONS TO ASK THE RECEPTION SITE COORDINATOR

Photocopy; use one for each location interviewed.

Reception site: _____

- What type of hall or social rooms are available? _____

- What is the maximum number their room can accommodate? _____

- What is the fee? _____

- For how many hours? _____

- Are there overtime charges? _____

- What is included? _____

- Do they provide tables, chairs, linens, china and silver? _____

- Is there any additional fee? _____

- Are there certain days of the week, or times of the day, when the price is discounted? _____

- Can the site be used for both the ceremony and reception? _____

- Can you use your own caterer or is there an in-house caterer that must be used? _____

- Are there music restrictions concerning the type of music or length of time it may be played? _____

- Is there a piano, or other musical instruments, at the site? Is there a charge to use them? _____

- Are there regulations on photography or video taping? _____

- Are there rooms available for the bride, groom and attendants to change into wedding attire or going-away clothes? _____

- Are there restrictions on alcohol? _____

- May hard liquor, beer, wine or champagne be served? _____

- May you provide your own liquor? _____

- With wine or champagne, is there a corkage fee? _____

- If they provide the liquor, what is the per drink or per person charge? _____

- Is there an adequate kitchen? _____

- Is there a dance floor? _____

- Do they provide a microphone? _____

- If outside, are there heaters and lights? _____

- If not, is there sufficient electrical power available to use them there? _____

- Are there adequate restroom facilities? _____

- Is liability insurance, including liquor liability, included in the rental fee? _____

- Do they provide a coat check? _____

- What is the fee, if any? _____

- Do they have adequate parking? _____

- Is there an additional fee? _____

- What is the deposit? _____

- What is the cancellation policy? _____

- If reception is to be in a garden, can the area be tented? _____

- Is there an alternative location that can accommodate the guests in the event of bad weather? _____

- With a private reception site, do neighbors, police or security companies need to be notified? _____

- Is there a special area for guests to wait for the arrival of the bride and groom? _____

- Is there a good location for the receiving line, guest book and gift tables? _____

- Is a security deposit required? _____

- If so, how much? _____

- When is it refunded? _____

- Is the clean-up included in the rental fee? _____

Planning the Reception

RECEPTION SITE WORKSHEET

	ESTIMATE #1		ESTIMATE #2	
	Name ___		Name ___	
	Phone ___		Phone ___	
	Description	**Cost**	**Description**	**Cost**
ROOM/HALL Date Available Time Occupancy Fee				
EQUIPMENT Tables Chairs Linens				
FOOD Hors d'oeuvres Buffet Sit-down Wedding Cake				
BEVERAGES Open bar Champagne/Wine Non-alcoholic				
NUMBER OF SERVERS Waiters Bartenders Valet Parkers Tips				
MISCELLANEOUS				
TOTAL				

	ESTIMATE #1	ESTIMATE #2
Gratuities included	☐ Yes ☐ No	☐ Yes ☐ No
Sales Tax Included	☐ Yes ☐ No	☐ Yes ☐ No
Number of Hours	___ hours	___ hours
Overtime Cost	___ per hour	___ per hour
Cancellation	Policy ___ Fee ___	Policy ___ Fee ___
Deposit Required	Amount ___ Date ___	Amount ___ Date ___

141

CATERERS

As tradition has it, some types of refreshments are served to celebrate after the wedding ceremony. It is customary to at least serve a wedding cake and punch, and to provide champagne with which to toast. Most people choose to serve something more than this, depending on the time of the reception and their budget. The food and beverage portion of the wedding is usually the greatest expense. Remember, the simplest or most elaborate reception can be wonderful if you plan carefully, use good taste and common sense.

If your reception is being held in a hotel, club or restaurant which does the catering, be sure to meet with the person in charge. Review the menu selections and services provided. Make sure the establishment has catered other weddings. If possible, taste the food before committing to the location.

Selecting a Caterer

When your reception is being held in a home, garden, or hall which allows you to provide a caterer of your choice, the options are numerous. Caterers' services and fees vary. Determine what your needs and desires are. Then interview several until you find one you feel confident can give you what you want. Good caterers are reserved months in advance. Start interviewing early and be prepared to leave a deposit in order to reserve your particular date and time.

When interviewing caterers find out what services they provide. Some companies specialize, and merely handle food preparation, delivery, and service. Some provide every service and take care of the details and coordination of your wedding, including food preparation and serving, all rental equipment, set up and clean up, liquor, beverages, bartenders, floral and other decorations. They may provide the cake or recommend a baker. They may also be helpful with suggestions of photographers and music coordinators. Other caterers may not provide all the above services, but may recommend competent people you can contract directly.

Most caterers have pictures of weddings they have done. Look at them, check their references or the Better Business Bureau, and taste their food before signing a contract. Read the contract carefully to be sure it includes everything you agreed on and states the total price, and check the cancellation policies. The catering fee is usually a flat fee based on the number of guests, or a fee per person, depending on the type and amount of food provided. A 15% service charge plus sales tax is usually added to the total. Be sure to check. You wouldn't want any surprises. Most require 50% to 75% of the money and a total guest count a week or two before the ceremony. Do not pay the balance until after the reception, and only if you are satisfied that you received what was agreed upon.

Selecting a Menu

Your caterer is the expert and will make menu suggestions to fit the style, budget and number of guests of your particular wedding. The time of day will determine what refreshments are appropriate.

A good caterer will be flexible and offer a variety of items with varying prices to enable you to serve something appropriate and stay within your budget. Serve chicken breast rather than filet mignon, or have a beautiful display of fruit or cheese rather than one of expensive shrimp and crab. Try to offer a variety so there will be something suitable for everyone's taste.

Use the following worksheets to help you select a caterer and record the menu you plan to serve.

QUESTIONS TO ASK YOUR CATERER

- What type of food items do you recommend for my budget and the number of guests? _____

- What type of service, sit-down dinner or buffet, would be best? _____

- Discuss menu selections, ask the cost per person. _____

- Do you provide linens? Is there an additional fee? _____

- Is there a color selection? _____

- Do you supply glasses, plates and silverware? _____

- Is there an additional charge? _____

- Do you handle all rental equipment such as tables, chairs, serving pieces? _____

- Would it cost less if I handle the rentals myself? _____

- How much time will you need to set up? _____

- Can we go over the table locations and seating arrangements ahead of time? _____

- Do you handle the clean up? Rental returns? _____

- Will you personally handle and attend my reception? _____

- If not, what is the name of the person who will? _____

- Do you make arrangements for flowers, decorations, and music? _____

- Do you provide the wedding cake? _____

- If not, is there a cake cutting fee? _____

- Do you charge extra to pour coffee? _____

- Will you provide the groom's cake, if we want one? _____

- Do you provide the liquor? _____

- What is the cost per drink? _____

- Is it cheaper if we provide our own liquor? _____

- Do you charge a corkage fee per bottle if we provide our own wine and champagne? _____

- Do you require a guaranteed number of guests? _____

- What is the last date I can give you a final guest count? _____

- Do you have a contract? _____

- When will you provide the final per person cost? _____

- What is the payment policy? _____

- What is the deposit to hold the date? _____

- What is your refund or cancellation policy? _____

- Are gratuities already figured in the total price? _____

- If so, what percent is being charged? _____

- Do you provide food for the photographer, videographer, or musicians? _____

- Is this an extra per person fee? _____

- Will you pack a to-go snack for the bride and groom? _____

- Will you pack the top tier of the wedding cake? _____

CATERER WORKSHEET

	ESTIMATE #1		ESTIMATE #2	
	Name _____		Name _____	
	Phone _____		Phone _____	
	Description	**Cost**	**Description**	**Cost**
FOOD				
Hors d'oeuvres				
Buffet				
Sit-down				
Wedding Cake				
BEVERAGES				
Alcohol				
Champagne/Wine				
Non-alcohol				
SERVICE				
Waiters				
Bartenders				
Valet				
EQUIPMENT				
Tables				
Chairs				
Linens				
Tent, etc.				
DECORATIONS				
Flowers				
Candles				
Etc.				
MISCELLANEOUS				
TOTAL				

	ESTIMATE #1	ESTIMATE #2
Gratuities included	☐ Yes ☐ No	☐ Yes ☐ No
Sales Tax Included	☐ Yes ☐ No	☐ Yes ☐ No
Number of Hours	_____ hours	_____ hours
Overtime Cost	_____ per hour	_____ per hour
Cancellation	Policy _____ Fee _____	Policy _____ Fee _____
Deposit Required	Amount _____ Date _____	Amount _____ Date _____

RECEPTION INFORMATION SHEET

RECEPTION SITE _____

Address _____

Site Coordinator _____ Phone _____

Confirmed Date _____ Time _____ to _____

Room Reserved _____

Deposit Amount _____ Date Due _____

Balance Amount _____ Date Due _____

Cancellation Policy _____

Last date to give final head count _____

NUMBER OF GUESTS: Invited _____ Confirmed _____

TYPE OF RECEPTION:

❑ Sit-Down   ❑ Buffet   ❑ Cocktails/Hor d'oeuvres

CATERER (when different from Reception Site):

Contact person _____ Phone _____

Confirmed date/time _____ Last date for final head count _____

RECEPTION COST:

Cost per person: Food _____ Beverage _____ Total _____

Number of confirmed guests   _____

Cost per person   _____

(Number of guests x cost per person) Subtotal   _____

Sales tax   _____

Gratuity   _____

(Site or equipment) Rental fee   _____

Other   _____

Total cost   _____

Less Deposit   _____

Balance Due   _____

EQUIPMENT CHECKLIST

Rental Company _____ Date Ordered _____

Address _____

Contact Person _____ Phone _____

Delivery Date/Time _____/_____ Pick-up date/time _____/_____

Cancellation Policy _____ Damaged/Broken policy _____

Item	Qty.	Cost
CEREMONY EQUIPMENT		
Aisle Runner (length)		
Aisle Stanchions		
Aisle Candelabra		
Free-standing		
Clamp style		
Altar candelabra		
No. of lights		
No. of lights		
Candles		
Size _____		
Candlelighter		
Canopy/Chuppah		
Flower stands		
Style_____ Size_____		
Style_____ Size_____		
Guestbook stand		
Kneeling bench		
Lattice backdrops		
Lattice arch		
Microphone		
Other _____		
CHAIRS		
Style _____		
TABLES		
Round tables		
36" seats 4 people		
48" seats 6 people		
60" seats 8 people		
72" seats 10 – 12 people		
Oblong tables		
6' seats 6 – 8 people		
8' seats 8 – 10 people		

Item	Qty.	Cost
Square tables		
34" square		
LINENS		
Round cloths – *Color*_____		
60" fits 24"– 36" table		
72" fits 24" to floor or 36"– 48" table		
90" fits 36" to floor or 48"– 60" table		
100" fits 48" to floor or 60"– 72" table		
Long cloth		
54" x 54" fits cardtable		
60" x 60" fits cardtable		
60" x 120" fits 6' and 8' tables		
NAPKINS		
Cocktail size		
Dinner size		
❑ *Paper* ❑ *Cloth* Color _____		
DINNERWARE		
❑ *China* ❑ *Paper*		
Dinner plates		
Salad plates		
Bread plates		
Luncheon plates		
Soup bowls		
Cake plates		
Coffee cups/saucers		
Demitasse cups/saucers		

Item	Qty.	Cost
FLATWARE		
❏ *Stainless* ❏ *Silverplate*		
Dinner knives	_____	_____
Steak knives	_____	_____
Butter knives	_____	_____
Dinner forks	_____	_____
Salad forks	_____	_____
Dessert forks	_____	_____
Teaspoons	_____	_____
Soup spoons	_____	_____
Demitasse spoons	_____	_____
Serving spoons	_____	_____
Meat forks	_____	_____
Cake knife/server	_____	_____
GLASSWARE		
❏ *Glass* ❏ *Plastic*		
Wine glasses	_____	_____
Champagne glasses	_____	_____
Water goblets	_____	_____
Highballs	_____	_____
Double rocks	_____	_____
Snifters	_____	_____
Water glasses	_____	_____
Punch cups	_____	_____
TRAYS		
❏ *Silverplate* ❏ *Plastic*		
Round 12"	_____	_____
Round 14"	_____	_____
Round 16"	_____	_____
Round 20"	_____	_____
Oval 13" x 21"	_____	_____
Oval 15" x 24"	_____	_____
Oblong 10" x 17"	_____	_____
Oblong 14" x 22"	_____	_____
Oblong 17" x 23"	_____	_____
Meat platters	_____	_____
Waiters' trays/stands	_____	_____
SERVING PIECES		
Chafing dish, 2 qt.	_____	_____
Chafing dish, 4 qt.	_____	_____
Chafing dish, 8 qt.	_____	_____

Item	Qty.	Cost
Bowls, 12"	_____	_____
Bowls, 16"	_____	_____
Bowls, 20"	_____	_____
Punch fountain, 3 gal.	_____	_____
Punch fountain, 7 gal.	_____	_____
Punch bowl, ladle	_____	_____
Coffee maker, 35 cup	_____	_____
Coffee maker, 50 cup	_____	_____
Coffee maker, 100 cup	_____	_____
Silver coffee and tea set	_____	_____
Insulated coffee pitcher	_____	_____
Creamer & sugar set	_____	_____
Sugar tongs	_____	_____
Salt & pepper set	_____	_____
Water pitchers	_____	_____
Ash trays	_____	_____
Table candles	_____	_____
MISCELLANEOUS EQUIPMENT		
Barbeque grill	_____	_____
Electric hotplate	_____	_____
Microwave	_____	_____
Portable bar	_____	_____
Ice chest	_____	_____
Coolers	_____	_____
Dance floor		
Size _____	_____	_____
Stage Platform	_____	_____
Lighting		
Twinkle lights	_____	_____
Tiki torches	_____	_____
Spot lights	_____	_____
Pole lights	_____	_____
Hurricane lights	_____	_____
Heaters	_____	_____
Fans	_____	_____
Extension cords	_____	_____
Tents/canopies		
Size _____	_____	_____
Umbrellas	_____	_____
Indoor/outdoor carpet		
Size _____	_____	_____

Item	Qty.	Cost
Trash cans/liners	_____	_____
Coat rack	_____	_____
Portable toilets	_____	_____
Electric bug zapper	_____	_____
Stands for table #s	_____	_____

BAR

Bottle/can openers	_____	_____
Corkscrews	_____	_____
Cocktail shakers	_____	_____
Strainers	_____	_____
Electric blender	_____	_____
Ice buckets	_____	_____
Ice tubs	_____	_____
Sharp knives	_____	_____
Tall spoons	_____	_____
Condiments tray	_____	_____

OTHER

_____	_____	_____
_____	_____	_____
_____	_____	_____
_____	_____	_____
_____	_____	_____
_____	_____	_____

Total Rental Cost _____

Deposit _____

Balance Due _____

RECEPTION SEATING CHART

BRIDE'S TABLE

Type and size of table _____

Number of chairs _____

Order of seating (list or diagram)

ATTENDANTS' TABLE

Type and size of table _____

Number of chairs _____

Order of seating (list or diagram)

PARENTS' TABLE

Type and size of table _____

Number of chairs _____

Order of seating (list or diagram)

PARENTS' TABLE

Type and size of table _____

Number of chairs _____

Order of seating (list or diagram)

SEATING CHART

Type & size of table _____

Number of chairs per table _____

TABLE # _____

_____ _____
_____ _____
_____ _____
_____ _____
_____ _____

TABLE # _____

_____ _____
_____ _____
_____ _____
_____ _____
_____ _____

TABLE # _____

_____ _____
_____ _____
_____ _____
_____ _____
_____ _____

TABLE # _____

_____ _____
_____ _____
_____ _____
_____ _____
_____ _____

TABLE # _____

_____ _____
_____ _____
_____ _____
_____ _____
_____ _____

TABLE # _____

_____ _____
_____ _____
_____ _____
_____ _____

TABLE # _____

_____ _____
_____ _____
_____ _____
_____ _____
_____ _____

TABLE # _____

_____ _____
_____ _____
_____ _____
_____ _____
_____ _____

TABLE # _____

_____ _____
_____ _____
_____ _____
_____ _____
_____ _____

TABLE # _____

_____ _____
_____ _____
_____ _____
_____ _____
_____ _____

TABLE # _____

_____ _____
_____ _____
_____ _____
_____ _____
_____ _____

TABLE # _____

_____ _____
_____ _____
_____ _____
_____ _____

Planning the Reception

TABLE # _____

_____ _____
_____ _____
_____ _____
_____ _____
_____ _____

TABLE # _____

_____ _____
_____ _____
_____ _____
_____ _____
_____ _____

TABLE # _____

_____ _____
_____ _____
_____ _____
_____ _____
_____ _____

TABLE # _____

_____ _____
_____ _____
_____ _____
_____ _____
_____ _____

TABLE # _____

_____ _____
_____ _____
_____ _____
_____ _____
_____

TABLE # _____

_____ _____
_____ _____
_____ _____
_____ _____
_____ _____

TABLE # _____

TABLE # _____

_____ _____
_____ _____
_____ _____
_____ _____
_____ _____

TABLE # _____

_____ _____
_____ _____
_____ _____
_____ _____

TABLE # _____

_____ _____
_____ _____
_____ _____
_____ _____
_____ _____

TABLE # _____

_____ _____
_____ _____
_____ _____
_____ _____

TABLE # _____

_____ _____
_____ _____
_____ _____
_____ _____

MENU WORKSHEET

Number of Guests _____

Reception Style: ❏ Sit-down   ❏ Buffet
                  ❏ Punch and cake   ❏ Cocktails/Hors d'oeuvres

HORS D'OEUVRES

_____

SALADS

_____

MAIN COURSE

_____

OTHER DISHES

_____

DESSERTS

_____

WEDDING CAKE

_____

BEVERAGES

BAKERIES

If your wedding cake is not supplied by the hotel, restaurant or your caterer, take time and care in choosing a baker. Your wedding cake is an important part of the wedding celebration. You will want it not only to look wonderful, but taste fabulous. Today there is a great variety to choose from. You may want to stay with something traditional or you may prefer something unusual and unique. Start looking early and get recommendations from friends or your caterer.

Check a number of bakers, discuss the various styles available and the prices. Many have pictures or actual cakes you can see, which will give you some good ideas. Ask if they can give you tasting samples. You will be able to determine the quality of the cake, and tasting will help you choose a flavor you like.

Types of Wedding Cake Bakers

Commercial Bakeries. Commercial bakeries are the most commonly used source for wedding cakes. Many specialize in nothing but wedding or special occasion cakes. These bakeries produce a large quantity of cakes, and generally have a variety of cake styles and designs to choose from. One disadvantage with this type of bakery is that they may not be able to deviate from their set designs, in the event you wanted something unique.

Caterer or Reception Site. Many times your caterer or reception location will provide the wedding cake. Since wedding cakes may not be their expertise, ask to see pictures and taste a cake you are considering. They may be limited in design ability, but then again, they may be great. By having your caterer or reception site provide the cake, the fee for cutting the cake is usually included in the price. It will probably be an extra charge if you choose to purchase a cake from another source.

Non-commercial Wedding Cake Bakers. This is a baker who usually works out of his or her home (or rents a small kitchen somewhere) and specializes in unique, creative wedding cakes. Each cake is individually designed to your specifications. Many of these bakers are true artists, and their love is to create spectacular cakes. The trend to use this type of baker has grown over the past few years, and prices vary widely. In some cases they can be less expensive than a commercial baker because of lower overhead; and in other cases they are more expensive, because of the elaborate detail and personalized design they offer. Finding this type of baker may also not be as easy as finding a commercial baker.

How to Find a Great Bakery

- Get recommendations from friends whose wedding cakes you have enjoyed.

- Ask your reception site coordinator which good bakeries they have worked with before.

- Your florist and photographer are also good sources because they usually see, and often taste, cakes at various weddings. They are in a position to hear who's good and who's not.

- Bridal magazines are also a source for you—many bakeries who specialize in wedding cakes will run regional ads in these national publications.

- Bridal fairs or shows are great places to see local bakeries' photographs and taste their cakes, since most will pass out small sample pieces.

Cake Flavors Available

Traditional wedding cakes have always been white, yellow or chocolate, with tiers frosted with a white butter cream frosting, then decorated with ribbon-like loops and pastel flowers. Although round cakes tend to be the most popular, square, rectangular and heart shapes are also used.

Today, a variety of flavors and fillings are used. If you prefer something out of the ordinary, make sure your baker can handle it. Popular flavors are carrot, German chocolate, chocolate mousse or chocolate cake with mocha filling. These may be frosted with a butter cream or freshly whipped cream. You may want a vanilla cake filled with lemon, raspberry, or vanilla custard. The choices are endless. Try to select something most people will like.

Decorations

The traditional frosting and decorations may be done on any cake and topped with a bride and groom. Many today are choosing to decorate their cakes with fresh or silk flowers. There are also a number of crystal or porcelain cake tops you may want to consider. They vary in price and style, so look around before deciding.

Ordering the Cake

Order your cake once you have selected your baker, determined the style, the flavor of the cake, the icing and filling, and the size, according to the number of guests it must serve. This should be done at least six to eight weeks before the wedding. Prepare to leave a deposit at this time. Be sure to get a receipt or contract listing all the particulars of your order including the date, the time, the location of the delivery, the total price with extras, if any, less the deposit, and the amount of the balance due.

The top layer of the wedding cake is saved to share on your first wedding anniversary. Make sure it is securely wrapped and immediately frozen. If you have toasting goblets, a bottle of champagne can be added for the celebration.

Groom's Cake

The traditional groom's cake has been a dark fruit cake which is cut into pieces and placed in boxes for the guests to take home. With the revival of this old tradition, many brides are adding a creative touch by opting for a chocolate layered cake in a variety of shapes representing a groom's favorite sport or hobby. These cakes are either being served at the reception along with the wedding cake, or following the old tradition, being placed in a box for the guests to take home. The legend is that a girl who places this cake under her pillow at night will dream of the man she will marry.

However, with the high cost of weddings these days, many brides choose to omit this tradition. This is perfectly acceptable.

SHOPPING TIPS

- Start interviewing wedding cake bakers about three to four months in advance.

- Look through the bridal magazines for pictures of cakes you like; take these with you when interviewing bakers.

- Ask to see photographs of wedding cakes they have created for other weddings.

- Ask if you can have a sample taste. Some bakers set aside a specific time, or day of the week, when samples of all their flavors are available for brides to taste.

- If you're planning a garden wedding, especially during the hottest part of summer, let your baker know. Some types of cakes and frostings hold up better than others in the heat.

- Discuss final details such as size, flavor of the frosting, decoration and set up.

- If fresh flowers are to be used on the cake, have your baker coordinate the details with your florist.

- Get a contract specifying the delivery date, time and place, the size, shape, flavor, any extras, total cost and the amount of your deposit.

Money Saving Tips

- **Hire an out-of-home baker**. Find a non-commercial baker who works out of his or her home, and whose overhead is lower.

- **Keep decorations simple**. Don't select a cake with extremely elaborate decorations, such as hand-made sugar lilies that look as if they have just been picked; opt for a simple design.

- **Add height by using styrofoam tiers**. If you love the look of a tall cake, but don't need to feed a lot of people, cut your cost by decorating styrofoam shapes and using them for two of the tiers.

- **Order an elaborate, smaller cake for the ceremonial cake-cutting.** Then have sheet cakes of the same recipe made to serve the guests.

- **Don't save the top tier**. Many couples save the top of their cake to eat on their first anniversary, then take one look at the cake a year later and, sad to say, toss it into the garbage. Time does not do much that's beneficial to the quality or appearance of the wedding cake. If, for reasons of tradition, you want to save something, keep just one or two pieces of the top tier. Or, for your anniversary, have a duplicate of the top tier made.

- **Order less cake**. If you are serving another dessert in addition to the wedding cake, or having a sweets table, plan on fewer servings of your cake and having smaller portions served.

- **Skip the groom's cake**. If you're working on a tight budget, eliminate the groom's cake. It's an old tradition, but one which will probably not be missed.

BAKERY WORKSHEET

	ESTIMATE #1		ESTIMATE #2	
	Name _____		Name _____	
	Phone _____		Phone _____	
	Description	**Cost**	**Description**	**Cost**
CAKE Size Shape No. of tiers				
CAKE FLAVORS				
FILLING FLAVORS				
ICING FLAVORS				
DECORATION				
GROOM'S CAKE				
TOTAL				

BAKERY SELECTED

Name _____   Order Date/Deposit _____

Address _____   Balance Due _____

Phone/Contact _____   Delivery Date/Time _____

CHAPTER TWELVE

Wedding Flowers

What would a wedding be without flowers? This traditional part of every wedding brings beauty, fragrance, and color to the event and adds that finishing touch to the ceremony and reception. Consider again the overall style and color scheme of your wedding. A creative florist who specializes in weddings can be a tremendous help. It is important he or she is experienced and, most of all, reliable.

SELECTING A FLORIST

Get recommendations from friends, your caterer, the hotel, or restaurant, and start interviewing florists at least two or three months in advance. Ask to look at pictures of other weddings they have done. Discuss with them the type of wedding you plan to have. It's helpful if they are familiar with the location. Select a florist that you feel comfortable with and that has the expertise to do the type of design you want, within your budget. (Use the shopping worksheets to help you.)

Once the decision has been made as to who this florist will be, go over the details with him or her. It is best to be prepared, have your budget in mind, swatches of fabric you're planning to use, a list of your favorite flowers or pictures of the type of look you want. This can help prevent disappointment later.

WHAT TYPE OF FLOWERS TO SELECT

Flowers that will be in season at the time of your wedding will be easier to get and less costly. This is not to say the others won't be available; with hothouse growing and shipping by air, you can get almost anything at any time – it just might cost you an arm and a leg.

The list below includes some favorite wedding flowers and their special meaning.

- Apple blossoms — good fortune
- Bluebells — constancy
- Blue violets — faithfulness
- Carnations — distinction
- Forget-me-nots — true love
- Gardenias — joy
- Lilies — purity and innocence
- Lily of the Valley — happiness
- Orange blossoms — purity and fertility
- Orchids — beauty
- Roses — love
- White daisies — innocence

FLOWER SUGGESTIONS

Amaryllis	Usually deep red, also available in white. Shaped similar to a lily with a long stem.	Spring, Winter. May be hard to get.
Anemones	Available in white, blue, red violet, yellow, Shaped similar to poppies.	Spring through Fall.
Asters	Usually available in white, pink, rose and purple.	Summer
Baby's Breath	Usually white. Fine delicate, tiny flowers.	Available year round through florists.
Bachelor Buttons	Available in white, pink, red, blue. They look like tiny carnations.	Summer
Calla Lily	White with yellow center. Unusual shape with long stems.	Spring through Fall
Canterbury Bells	Usually blue, purple or pink. Shaped like little bells.	Summer
Carnations	Available in many colors. Very fragrant. A commonly known flower.	Available year round. Usually inexpensive.
Catlaya Orchids	Usually white with shades of pink or lavender in the center of each petal. Larger than other orchids.	Available through florist year round. Very experience.
Chrysanthemum	Available in white, yellow, red. They come in many shaped and sizes.	Summer to Winter
Daffodils	Available in many colors. A pretty flower which is very common.	Spring
Daisies	Usually white or yellow with yellow center. A popular flower similar, but smaller than a chrysanthemum.	Summer through Fall. Inexpensive in season.
Day Lily	Usually in shades of cream, orange, red, yellow with a variety of stem lengths.	Spring through Fall.
Delphinium	Usually in white, rose, lavender, blue. Long spikes of flowers with lacy foliage.	Spring through Fall
Forget-me-not	Dainty blue flower with yellow or white centers. Very pretty.	Spring
Gardenias	Pretty white flower with dark green leaves. Very fragrant.	Spring
Iris	Available in white, blue, violet, yellow and orange. Long stalks, large petals with two that drop down a little.	Spring through Summer
Lilac	Usually white or lavender. Stalks with many tiny flowers. Very fragrant.	Spring
Lily	Usually white or cream with tinges of pink or lavender.	Spring through Summer
Lily of the Valley	White flowers. Bell-shaped and clustered on a long spike stem. Very fragrant and delicate.	Spring
Orchid	Usually white, or in shades of pink or lavender. Popular and common flower.	Available year round through florist
Roses	Available in a number of colors. A bud at the end of a long, thorned stem. Buds vary in size down to a miniature rose with a bud of less than 1 inch. Very popular and fragrant.	Summer is their season, but available year round through florist.
Spray Orchid	Long spikes covered with tiny orchid-like flowers.	Winter. Very expensive.
Stephanotis	These are white trumpet-shaped flowers which grow on vines. Popular in bouquets and have a sweet fragrance.	Summer
Straw Flowers	Available in white, yellow, orange, red. Straw-like petals shaped like daisies.	Summer
Violets	Available in white, blue, purple. Tiny flowers with a nice fragrance.	Spring
Zephyr Lily	Available in white, yellow and shades of pink. Smaller than most lilies.	Summer through Fall

FLOWERS FOR THE BRIDAL PARTY

The bridal flowers may vary from a large bouquet to a single flower, but, for tradition, the bride and her attendants should carry something. It not only adds to the overall beauty, but gives a nervous bride a graceful place to put her hands. Large bouquets can be heavy; be careful not to overcompensate by holding them up too high. Your lower arm should rest on the top of the hipbones.

Bridal Bouquets

Among all the shapes and types of flowers available, you should find something perfect for you, and the gown you have selected, with the help of a good florist. For a petite bride or a very ornate gown, a smaller, more simple bouquet would be in order. With a larger or tall bride and a less elaborate gown, a beautiful cascading bouquet would balance nicely.

Other ideas to consider would be an heirloom fan or family Bible decorated with a flower or two and satin ribbons. For an old-fashioned Victorian look carry a nosegay or a flower-filled basket. If it's a dramatic contemporary look you want to achieve, try a long-stemmed arrangement of calla lilies wrapped with white or colored satin ribbon, and carried over the arm as you walk down the aisle.

Some florists will give you a smaller "throwing" bouquet, or you may want to purchase one in order to keep yours for preserving.

Bridesmaids' and Maid of Honor's Flowers

The bridesmaids' bouquets are generally smaller and should coordinate with the bridal bouquet. The size and color should complement their dresses and the overall look of the wedding. The maid or matron of honor's bouquet may be of a different color, depending on her dress, or larger in size to set her apart from the others.

Flower Girl

Most flower girls wear a delicate wreath and carry a nosegay or small basket decorated with flowers and colored ribbons. The basket is filled with rose petals to be scattered in the path of the bride. If this is prohibited in your place of worship, have her hand a single rose to guests as she walks down the aisle.

Hairpieces

You may decide to wear flowers in your hair rather than another type of headpiece. They may be worn alone or as a delicate wreath with a veil attached to the back. For a second-time bride who is not to wear a veil, a nice look is a flat white orchid worn on the side of the head, alone or with thin white satin ribbons to add that delicate touch. Make sure they are securely fastened.

Mothers and Grandmothers

Both of your mothers and grandmothers should be presented a corsage to either pin on their dress or handbag; or, if preferred, they may wear the corsage around a wrist. Check to see which style they would prefer, or if a special color is needed to coordinate with their dresses. In addition to, or in place of, a corsage you may want to add more sentiment by giving each of your mothers a rose from your bouquet once you have reached the end of the aisle.

Groom, Fathers, and Ushers

All of the men traditionally wear boutonnieres, generally a single blossom such as a rosebud or shaft of lilies of the valley. All of the men's boutonnieres are alike except for the groom's. He wears something a little special.

Ringbearer

The ringbearer may or may not wear a boutonniere. It depends on his outfit. With a tuxedo you may want him to wear a boutonniere, whereas with knickers and knee socks it may not be appropriate.

FLOWERS FOR THE CEREMONY

There are a number of designs and types of flowers to use. Before you start making definite decisions, check to see if your church or synagogue has any regulations or restrictions regarding them.

The types of arrangements should be determined by the size and lighting of the church, the season, and the colors of your wedding. For example, in a large church with a high ceiling a larger arrangement using bolder flowers is best. The purpose of flowers at a church ceremony is to direct visual attention toward the front of the church and to the bridal couple. Therefore, they also need to be seen by the guests seated in the back.

In elaborate, formal weddings with larger budgets, flowers and ribbons are draped down the aisle to mark the pews and add color. When cost is a concern, this is one place to cut down. Either use live flowers in decorative baskets at the altar, or to line the aisle. Another cost-saving idea, which can be done if the ceremony and reception are held in the same location, is to use table centerpieces on both sides of the altar or place them down the aisle.

In a Jewish ceremony the vows are said under a chuppah which is placed at the altar and covered with greens and fresh flowers. For outdoor ceremonies decorated arches are always popular. Your florist may have some great ideas!

Make sure you have a written contract that includes the arrival time and date, with the total price. You will probably have to give a deposit but do not pay in full until all the flowers have been delivered.

FLOWERS FOR THE RECEPTION

The flowers for the reception, like everything else, should fit your style and color scheme. Most reception flowers include table decorations which can be cut flowers, beautifully arranged in baskets or placed around a center candle. The arrangements should complement the table linens and the size of the table. To keep the cost down and for less formal receptions, use small potted flowering plants placed in white baskets, or consider using dried or silk arrangements that you could make yourself and give later as gifts.

If buffet tables are used, it is nice to have some type of flower arrangement which adds color and overall beauty. It can help transform a stark reception hall into a warm, colorful room. In addition, consider renting indoor plants or small trees to achieve a garden effect.

Special Touches

Other added touches which can make a reception room, home or garden into a warm romantic setting for an evening reception:

- Use a tall center candle alone or complemented by small votive candles placed around it; have the other lights dim.

- Use the votive candles in other places, such as along walkways, around a pool, or in the bathrooms.

- Use twinkle lights to add that magical feeling to a room, or especially to a garden. If small trees are brought in to warm up a reception hall, add some twinkle lights to them.

PRESERVING YOUR BOUQUET

If you're a bride who wants to keep your bouquet for sentimental reasons, make sure you order a "throwing" bouquet.

Ask your florist about preserving the bridal bouquet for you. It can be displayed in a shadow box or put under a glass case. The moisture is removed; then it is sprayed with a protective solution.

The preserving process may also be done yourself by placing your bouquet in a box and completely covering it with borax or silica gel. This process usually takes about a week.

Pressing

This is another method, which takes about six weeks and is commonly used if the bouquet is to be framed. Separate the bouquet, place it between newspapers and cover it with books or heavy objects.

Potpourri

This method is a great idea. Preserve the bouquet and place it in a glass jar or box and have the wedding date inscribed on it, or put it in a sachet pouch. Once the petals have been removed and individually dried, which can be done by placing them on a cookie sheet at a warm temperature in your oven, mix in the following herbs and spices for a nice fragrance: mint, bay leaves, lemon balm, or cinnamon and fruit peels. Then add a few drops of jasmine, rose, or geranium oil (can be purchased in drugstores). The fragrance will intensify over time.

Drying Rose Petals

If rice is not allowed or preferred, have friends help you collect rose petals the months before the wedding. Dry the petals individually by placing them on a cookie sheet at a warm temperature in your oven. Store them in plastic bags until the wedding day (you may add a few drops of jasmine, rose or geranium oil for fragrance). The day of the wedding they can be placed in silver bowls, and handfuls passed out to the guests. Or you may want to wrap the petals in 6" circles of nylon netting gathered with a satin ribbon, which may be placed at each table setting or passed to guests just before the bridal couple's departure.

Colored Rice

If the traditional rice is to be thrown, why not add a little color to it! Simply mix one cup of water with 1/2 to 1 teaspoon of food coloring (depending upon how much color you want). Add 1 ½ cups of uncooked rice, let stand for five minutes. Drain, then spread the rice in the bottom of a baking pan and place in 250° pre-heated oven for 15 minutes. Stir occasionally, remove and place on paper towels to dry. Colored water may be used for a second batch. Each batch will fill thirty-six 6" circles of nylon netting which can be gathered with a satin ribbon.

MONEY SAVING TIPS

- **Share floral cost with another bride**. Find out if there will be another wedding at your church or synagogue on the same day. Possibly you can arrange to share the cost of floral decorations.

- **Use flowers in season**. Avoid exotic, expensive flowers that may have to be imported, or flowers that are not in season.

- **Decorate with greenery**. Use greenery such as trees and garlands of ivy to fill large areas. It can give a dramatic impact for relatively little money. Small trees can usually be rented.

Wedding Flowers

- **Have a garden wedding**. Consider having the ceremony and/or the reception in a beautiful garden, surrounded by natural flowers.

- **Don't plan your wedding to be held near a holiday**. Flowers traditionally will be more expensive and scarce at this time, especially Valentine's Day and Mother's Day. Planning it around Christmas, on the other hand, might save you some money since many reception locations will already be decorated for the holiday season.

- **Limit your attendants**. Limit the number of attendants you have in your wedding party. Obviously, the fewer attendants, the fewer the number of bouquets you'll need to buy.

- **Use balloons**. Balloons are an inexpensive way of adding color to a reception site; they are especially effective for a larger room with high ceilings.

- **Re-use the arrangements and bouquets**. Use the same floral arrangements for both the ceremony and reception; this is made easier when they are both in the same location. Floral table arrangements can be used to line the aisle, or may be grouped together and placed on each side of the altar. Bouquets can also be used to decorate the cake and guest book table.

- **Consider smaller bouquets**. Rather than having you and your bridesmaids carry large, expensive bouquets, choose to carry small, elegant bouquets. Or, consider the dramatic look of one or two calla lilies whose stems are wrapped with a beautiful ribbon bow.

FLORAL CHECKLIST

Florist _____ Date Ordered _____

Contact Person _____ Phone _____

| *Qty:* | *Item:* | *Description (style, color, flowers):* | *Cost:* |

BRIDE:

_____ Bouquet _____ _____

_____ Bride's Throwing Bouquet _____ _____

_____ Floral Headdress for reception _____ _____

_____ Going-away Corsage _____ _____

Delivered to _____Time _____ _____

BRIDAL ATTENDANTS:

_____ Matron of Honor _____ _____

_____ Maid of Honor _____ _____

_____ Bridesmaids _____ _____

_____ Flower Girl_____ _____

_____ Floral Headdresses _____ _____

Delivered to _____Time _____ _____

GROOM AND ATTENDANTS:

_____ Groom's boutonniere _____ _____

_____ Best Man's boutonniere _____ _____

_____ Ushers' boutonnieres _____ _____

_____ Ringbearer's boutonniere _____ _____

Delivered to _____Time _____ _____

Bridal Party Total: _____

FAMILY:

_____ Corsage for Bride's mother _____ _____

_____ Corsage for Groom's mother _____ _____

_____ Corsages for grandmothers _____ _____

_____ Mothers' roses _____ _____

FLORAL CHECKLIST (cont.)

_____ Other corsages (stepmothers, aunts) _____ _____

_____ Boutonniere for Bride's father _____ _____

_____ Boutonniere for Groom's father _____ _____

_____ Other boutonnieres (stepfathers, grandfathers) _____ _____

Delivered to _____ Time _____ _____

Family Total: _____

FLOWERS FOR HELPERS:

_____ Bridal consultant _____ _____

_____ Officiant _____ _____

_____ Soloist _____ _____

_____ Instrumentalist(s) _____ _____

_____ Guest Book attendant _____ _____

_____ Gift attendant _____ _____

_____ Others _____ _____

Helpers Total: _____

CEREMONY SITE:

_____ Arch/Canopy _____ _____

_____ Candelabra _____ _____

_____ Candelighters _____ _____

_____ Altar floral sprays _____ _____

_____ Pews _____ _____

_____ Aisles _____ _____

_____ Other _____ _____

Ceremony Site Total: _____

RECEPTION SITE:

_____ Bride's table _____ _____

_____ Parents' table _____ _____

_____ Attendants' tables _____ _____

_____ Guests' tables _____ _____

FLORAL CHECKLIST (cont.)

_____ Cake table _____ _____

_____ Top of Cake _____ _____

_____ Guest Book table _____ _____

_____ Gift table _____ _____

_____ Ladies' Powder Room _____ _____

_____ Other _____ _____

Reception Site Total _____

(Total of all Categories) Subtotal _____

Sales Tax _____

Grand Total _____

Deposit _____

Balance Due _____

DUTIES:

Person responsible for distributing flowers to bridal party: _____

Person responsible for taking ceremony flowers to reception site: _____

Person responsible for taking reception flowers after reception: _____

     To be taken to: _____

Person responsible for having bouquet preserved: _____

Rental equipment to be returned to florist by: _____ or, picked-up on _____ at _____

CHAPTER THIRTEEN

Wedding Music

Music is a major part of your wedding and reception, and should be planned and selected carefully. Music helps create the atmosphere. Special songs will make the wedding uniquely your own. The music should be determined by you and your fiancé, keeping in mind the type of guests attending, the budget you have to work with, and any restrictions of the church or reception site.

Usually two different types of music are desired: softer, more romantic music sung or played during the ceremony, and entertaining or dancing music played for the reception. In some cases the same musicians may play both types. This is more common if the wedding and reception are in the same location. The alternative is to have one set of musicians or the church organist and soloist for the ceremony, and another group to play for the reception.

CEREMONY MUSIC

Before making any definite music arrangements or selections, you should check with your church or synagogue to see what restrictions it may have. Today there is a wonderful variety of music. Combinations of instruments are available, such as harps and violins. You are not limited to only a soloist or organist.

The music should start about a half hour before the ceremony, usually instrumentals to set the mood, with a solo sung just after the mother of the bride is seated. This lets people know the processional is about to start. The processional will begin usually with an instrumental, sometimes a solo, which has a good regular beat to walk to. Once the attendants have reached the altar, music which announces the bride is played, commanding everyone's attention as you walk down the aisle. This selection can be traditional or contemporary and either an instrumental or a solo. One or two songs may be played during the ceremony – any more would be too many. Finally there is the recessional, which should be more upbeat and a slightly quicker tempo. Music ideas are included at the end of this chapter.

RECEPTION MUSIC

Reception music can be any of a variety of types, depending on the mood you want set at that particular time. You may want something a little softer for the first hour during the receiving line or cocktails, and then have the tempo pick up as the evening goes on. Or maybe you prefer only violins, with no dancing. The types of musicians may range from an individual like a pianist, to a small combo of mixed instruments, to a larger orchestra of 8 to 20 people.

Don't forget the ages of your guests; try to select musicians that can play a variety of songs from slower traditional, to 50s and rock and roll, to faster contemporary music for dancing. It's a good idea to make a list of songs you would like played and give it to the band leader. Try to have a good mix of fast and slow songs. I'm sure the band leader will be able to help you arrange and select appropriate songs, if needed. Also go over

with him the timing of important announcements, such as the grand entrance, the first dance, cutting the cake, and throwing the bouquet and garter.

SELECTING THE MUSICIANS

Selecting your musicians and music carefully is important. It can add or detract from the success of your wedding and reception.

You may find musicians by asking friends or relatives, caterers, wedding consultants, your clergyman, or through the yellow pages or musicians' union in your area. If the reception is held in a hotel or restaurant, the manager may be helpful with music suggestions.

Make sure to interview a few groups before making a final decision. Ask to hear them play. You may do that at one of their events, or most bands today have a video of themselves, which is helpful. Discuss the fee, how many hours they will play, how many and how long their breaks will be and what they will wear. Check to see if they have recorded music which can be played during the breaks. Also make sure there are enough electrical outlets for their needs.

Make your musical arrangements as far in advance as possible. Give the musician a deposit to secure the date and get everything agreed upon in a written contract.

RECORDED MUSIC

Recorded music is becoming more popular today than ever before. There are a number of reasons for this. First, the equipment and the people operating it have gotten much more professional. With the cost of live music so high, it's an economical alternative at about half the price. Other advantages are that it provides continued music, and the space requirements are minimal. Recorded music also provides a wide variety, everything from classical, big band, country western, and rock and roll to the latest disco. The music may be pre-recorded on a reel-to-reel tape, or records may be used with a disc jockey who acts as master of ceremonies.

MONEY SAVING TIPS

- **Hire a professional disc jockey**. You can usually get continuous music for less than the cost of a band. The equipment used today provides a much better sound than in the past, and disc jockeys have gotten more professional.

- **Use pre-recorded music.** Pre-recorded music for the ceremony can also be purchased. Check restrictions, and equipment available, with your church or synagogue ahead of time.

- **Have a friend sing**. If you have friends who sing or play instruments such as organ, guitar or harp, ask them to play or sing at your ceremony.

- **Hire fewer musicians**. To keep costs down when you want live music at the reception, opt for a band with fewer musicians or hire a single performer.

MUSIC IDEAS

The following are favorite songs which may help you in making your selections. List these or others of your choice. Write your selections on the music list provided. A copy should be given to the band leader.

Music for the Ceremony

Bridal Chorus - Lohengrin's
 (*Here Comes the Bride*)

Wedding March - Mendelssohn's
 (Midsummer Night's Dream)

Wedding March - Alexander Guilmant

The Lord's Prayer - Malotte

The Wedding Song - Peter, Paul and Mary

Evergreen - Barbra Streisand

The Hawaiian Wedding Song - Andy Williams

Three Times a Lady - Commodores

Lady - Kenny Rogers

First Time Ever I Saw Your Face - Roberta Flack

Loving You - Minnie Ripperton

Sunrise, Sunset - from Fiddler on the Roof
 soundtrack

Music for the Receiving Line, Reception and First Dance

You Are So Beautiful to Me - Joe Cocker

You've Made Me So Very Happy - Blood, Sweat
 and Tears

We've Only Just Begun - Carpenters

Beginnings - Chicago

Feelings - Morris Albert

Longer - Dan Fogelberg

Truly - Lionel Ritchie

Beautiful - Gordon Lightfoot

Misty - Johnny Mathis

Chances Are - Johnny Mathis

That's All - Johnny Mathis

Endless Love - Diana Ross and Lionel Ritchie

I Only Have Eyes for You - Art Garfunkle

Unforgettable - Nat King Cole

I Love You So - McDonald and Chevalier

Waiting For A Girl Like You - Foreigner

Up Where We Belong - Joe Cocker

In the Mood - Glenn Miller

New York, New York - Frank Sinatra

Theme from Ice Castles - Melissa Manchester

Because of You - Tony Bennett

Love Theme from The Godfather - Andy Williams

Arthur's Theme - Christopher Cross

I Could Have Danced All Night - Anne Murray

When I Fall in Love - Lettermen

You Are the Sunshine of My Life - Stevie Wonder

On the Wings of Love - Jeffrey Osborne

Can't Help Falling in Love - Elvis Presley

Try to Remember - Harry Belafonte

Only You - The Platters

Colour My World - Chicago

You Light Up My Life - Debby Boone

I Love You Just the Way You Are - Billy Joel

And I Love You So - McLean

The Hands of Time (Brian's Song) - Michel LaGrand

Hopelessly Devoted To You - Olivia Newton John

More - Ortolani and Oliviero

Love Song - Anne Murray

Our Love - Carpenters

I Just Want to be Your Everything - Andy Gibb

What Are You Doing the Rest of Your Life - Michel LaGrand

Annie's Song - John Denver

Top of the World - Carpenters

The Song Is Love - Peter, Paul and Mary

I Won't Last A Day Without You - Andy Williams

A Love Song - Kenny Loggins

Time In A Bottle - Jim Croce

Till There Was You - Beatles

In My Life - Beatles

A Time For Us - Snyder

Sunshine On My Shoulders - John Denver

Sound of Music - Rodgers and Hammerstein

Sometimes - Henry Mancini

People - Barbra Streisand

Love Is A Many Splendored Thing - Percy Faith

This Is The Day - Brown

Through the Eyes of Love - Sager/Hamlisch

A Whole New World - Peabo Bryson and Regine Belle

Beauty and the Beast - Peabo Bryson and Celine Dion

I Will Always Love You - Whitney Houston

Hero - Mariah Carey

Have I Told You Lately - Rod Stewart

Wonderful Tonight - Eric Clapton

Save the Best for Last - Vanessa Williams

Everything I Do, I Do It for You - Bryan Adams

Unforgettable - Natalie Cole

When a Man Love a Woman - Michael Bolton

Through the Eyes of Love - Melissa Manchester

Love Won't Let Me Wait - Luther Vandross

Masterpiece - Atlantic Star

Endless Love - Luther Vandross and Mariah Carey

Can You Feel the Love Tonight - Elton John

MUSIC ESTIMATES

NUMBER OF HOURS NEEDED: *Ceremony* _____ *Reception* _____

CHOICE # _____   Music for: Ceremony ❏   Reception ❏

Agent/contact _____ Phone _____

Number of Musicians _____ Rate per hour _____ Overtime rate _____

Number of breaks _____ Length of breaks _____

Audition Date _____ Time _____ Location _____

Comments: _____

CHOICE # _____   Music for: Ceremony ❏   Reception ❏

Agent/contact _____ Phone _____

Number of Musicians _____ Rate per hour _____ Overtime rate _____

Number of breaks _____ Length of breaks _____

Audition Date _____ Time _____ Location _____

Comments: _____

CHOICE # _____   Music for: Ceremony ❏   Reception ❏

Agent/contact _____ Phone _____

Number of Musicians _____ Rate per hour _____ Overtime rate _____

Number of breaks _____ Length of breaks _____

Audition Date _____ Time _____ Location _____

Comments: _____

CHOICE # _____   Music for: Ceremony ❏   Reception ❏

Agent/contact _____ Phone _____

Number of Musicians _____ Rate per hour _____ Overtime rate _____

Number of breaks _____ Length of breaks _____

Audition Date _____ Time _____ Location _____

Comments: _____

CHOICE # _____   Music for: Ceremony ❏   Reception ❏

Agent/contact _____ Phone _____

Number of Musicians _____ Rate per hour _____ Overtime rate _____

Number of breaks _____ Length of breaks _____

Audition Date _____ Time _____ Location _____

Comments: _____

CEREMONY MUSIC INFORMATION

CEREMONY MUSICIANS SELECTED

Ceremony location _____

Contact person _____ Phone _____

Wedding date _____ Arrival time _____

Appropriate Dress _____

Rehearsal date _____ Time _____ Location _____

INSTRUMENTALISTS: *Phone*   *Fee*

_____   _____   _____

_____   _____   _____

_____   _____   _____

_____   _____   _____

_____   _____   _____

SOLOISTS: *Phone*   *Fee*

_____   _____   _____

_____   _____   _____

_____   _____   _____

Cancellation Policy: _____ **Total Cost** _____

_____ **Deposit Paid** _____

_____ **Balance Due** _____

CEREMONY MUSIC SELECTIONS

Prelude _____   During Ceremony _____

_____   _____

_____   _____

First Solo _____   _____

_____   _____

Second Solo _____   Recessional _____

_____

Processional _____   Postlude _____

_____

Notes _____

_____

RECEPTION MUSIC INFORMATION

RECEPTION MUSICIANS SELECTED

Reception location _____

Contact person _____ Phone _____

Reception date _____ Arrival time _____

Appropriate Dress _____

	Phone	*Fee*
Disc Jockey _____	_____	_____
Agent/Bandleader _____	_____	_____
Name of Band _____	_____	_____
Key Band Members _____	_____	_____
_____	_____	_____
_____	_____	_____
_____	_____	_____
_____	_____	_____

Cancellation Policy: _____ **Total Cost** _____

_____ **Deposit Paid** _____

_____ **Balance Due** _____

RECEPTION MUSIC SELECTIONS

Newlyweds' Arrival _____   Ethnic Dances _____

Receiving Line _____   _____

_____   _____

First Dance _____   Cake Cutting _____

Dancing or Background Music _____   Bouquet Toss _____

_____   Garter Toss _____

_____   Newlyweds' Get-Away _____

_____   _____

_____   Last Dance _____

_____   Other _____

_____   _____

_____   _____

Notes

_____

_____

_____

_____

_____

_____

_____

_____

_____

_____

_____

_____

_____

_____

_____

_____

_____

_____

_____

_____

_____

_____

_____

CHAPTER FOURTEEN

Photography and Videography

Your wedding photographs will need to capture the feelings, expressions and moments of yourspecial day. They will bring you years of pleasure, so select your professional photographer carefully. Most good photographers are in demand, especially in summer months, so start interviewing them as early as possible. You may get recommendations from your friends, caterer, florist, or clergyman.

SELECTING A PHOTOGRAPHER

Make sure, when interviewing a photographer, that you see his or her portfolio to determine if the style suits yours. Other things to look for are:

- Do the pictures have good color and clarity ?

- Did he pay attention to detail?

- Does he capture the emotions and expressions of the day?

- Is he creative with various poses?

- Does he use soft lenses and lighting?

- Can he do multiple exposures and split framing, which make interesting pictures?

Look at other wedding albums he has done. They may give you ideas for your own. See if each album is well balanced, with traditional and candid shots covering both wedding and reception. If you are considering taking formal portraits a few weeks before the ceremony, discuss this at the same time. These are generally taken in the photographer's studio where he has necessary lighting, backdrops and equipment. Wear your hair and accessories the same way you will on your wedding day.

TIPS FOR CHOOSING A PHOTOGRAPHER

- Start looking for a photographer six to nine months before your wedding, since many are booked months in advance.

- Look through the wedding albums of friends and relatives who live in your area. Personal recommendations are always good.

- Bridal fairs are a great place to see the work of various photographers; get the names of those whose style you like.

- Ask for recommendations from caterers, florists, or reception site coordinators.

- Interview several photographers by making appointments to review their work.

- Ask to see sample wedding albums or a set of proofs from a recent wedding.

- Be sure the photographers you contact specialize in weddings. Don't hire a commercial or part-time photographer who occasionally handles weddings.

- When looking at the sample albums, see if the photographer used different types of lighting

and whether he varied the backgrounds.

- Look for diversity in the poses. Does he seem to capture the personality of the bride and groom and the mood of their wedding?

- Consider the personality of each photographer; choose the one you feel is most competent and whose personality will make you and your guests feel most comfortable.

- Get every aspect of the agreement with the photographer in a written contract. The contract should include: the date, arrival time, length of shooting time, fees and overtime charges, if any. List all locations – the bride's home, ceremony and reception, giving addresses and directions. Include the cost and details of a photo package selection, and cost of additional photos you may want to order.

- Don't forget: If you're planning to send an announcement of your wedding to the newspaper, be sure your photographer knows, and takes a black and white portrait of the two of you as husband and wife. Order an 8 x 10 inch black and white glossy print to send to the paper.

PHOTOGRAHER'S FEE

When interviewing a photographer, be sure to discuss the number of pictures he takes, the cost of each print, the style and cost of the albums he offers, and whether there are travel costs or extra fees included. Photographers' fees can vary tremendously. Use the forms included in the back of this section to make accurate comparisons.

Most photographers that do a number of weddings offer a package, which is a predetermined number of pictures in various sizes for a set fee that includes the prints and the album. Generally pictures are less expensive when ordered this way. Check to see if packages are available for parents' albums.

Ask if he keeps the negatives and for how long. See if they can be purchased now or in the future. They should be kept in a fireproof safe, in the event your pictures are ever destroyed.

WHEN TO TAKE THE PICTURES

Have the photographer arrive at least an hour before the ceremony. You may want pictures while getting dressed, and of guests arriving. If the ceremony and reception are to be in the same location, you may want to take your formal, posed pictures before the guests arrive. If you do not want the groom to see you until the ceremony, then take as many pictures as you can without the two of you together before, and finish the remainder after the ceremony.

Make sure you get a written contract which specifies the time he is to arrive, the number of pictures he is to take, and how long he is to stay. Make sure he doesn't miss the cutting of the cake, the tossing of the bouquet and garter, or your leaving the reception .

ITEMS FOR THE PORTRAIT SESSION

- Wedding dress.
- Hat, headpiece and veil.
- Gloves, if any.
- Wedding shoes and stockings.
- Appropriate undergarments.
- Jewelry to be worn.
- Bible, hanky, garter and bouquet, if not furnished by photographer, but desired.

NEW TRENDS IN WEDDING PHOTOS

- **Before or After:** More couples are setting aside tradition, and choosing to have their formal wedding pictures taken before the ceremony. This prevents the photographer from having to rush, and the guests from having to wait for the bride and groom at the reception. Hair and makeup are fresh.

- **More Candids, Fewer Posed:** There's a big movement in wedding photography toward more candid shots and less posed pictures. Formal groupings of the bride and groom with their families and attendants are still the norm, but shots of family and guests at the reception are spontaneous and candid, rather than posed.

- **Black and White Photos:** Some couples are choosing to have photographs shot in both color and black and white, thus giving them the option to order some prints in color and others in black and white. Black and white is an old classic look and its popularity is coming back.

- **Double Exposures or Special Filters:** Soft, romantic portraits can be taken with the use of special filters or lenses. Popular today are portraits where other images, such as water, mountains, a candle or champagne glass, may be in the background.

CREATIVE PHOTO IDEAS

- On the guest book table, set around the room, or mounted on the wall, display a few photos of the bride and groom from birth to marriage. You might also include the wedding pictures of both sets of parents.

- Have Polaroid pictures taken of each guest alone, or with the bride and groom, to give as a favor before they leave.

- Place a throw-away camera on each table. Instruct the guests to take pictures during the reception. It will not only be entertaining, but you'll get a lot of great candid shots. Don't forget to arrange for someone to collect all the cameras at the end of the reception.

- You may want to check on sending a photo invitation.

- Thank-you notes with your wedding picture can be unique and a nice remembrance.

- Picture thank-you notes can be ordered from Kodak. A picture of you opening the guest's gift can be a nice thank you.

- Keep a camera with you throughout your planning and make a nice pre-wedding album. Capture the following moments: buying your rings, trying on dresses for yourself and the bridesmaids, addressing and mailing invitations, showers, a picture of getting your marriage license. Remember the fun of planning your wedding.

- Order extra pictures for special friends.

- Don't forget your honeymoon photo album. Be sure to pack your camera.

- Have a friend take Polaroid pictures of your wedding day. You can take the pictures along on your honeymoon.

- Make sure you don't have suntan lines, or that your face does not get sunburned. A red face will not look attractive in the pictures.

MONEY SAVING TIPS

- **Some photographers who work out of their homes offer lower prices**. Because their overhead is lower, they are able to pass these savings on to you.

- **Don't order the fancy leather upgrade album**. Either take the standard album, or see if you can order the package without the album and receive a discount. You may get an album as a wedding gift.

- **Opt for a less popular time**. Check the photographers' price structure. Some may agree to shoot your wedding for less if it's on Friday night or Saturday morning, when they are not as busy as on Saturday afternoon or evening.

- **A word of caution**: Be careful when trying to cut costs on photography. I recommend using a professional wedding photographer for at least the ceremony pictures. These pictures represent lasting memories you'll want to share with family and friends for years to come. Some brides have been extremely disappointed when a professional wasn't used. Don't forget – when the day's over, it's too late to do anything about bad pictures.

WHAT TO ASK YOUR PHOTOGRAPHER

- Will he personally be taking the photographs of your wedding? If not, ask to meet the person who will be. _____

- Does he work with an assistant and will he have back-up equipment in the event of a problem? _____

- Is he familiar with your ceremony and reception location? _____

- Can you give him a list of special people with whom you want pictures? _____

- How many hours does his price include? _____

- What's the charge, if any, if the reception should last longer than planned? _____

- Will he stay through the cake cutting and garter toss? _____

- How much time will you need to allow for the formal wedding photos taken either before or after the ceremony? _____

- What are the photo package prices? _____

- What are the individual picture prices? _____

- What about parents' albums? _____

- When will the proof pictures be ready? _____

- How long will the prints take, once they have been ordered? _____

- Will he sell the album or negatives? _____

- How many years does he keep the negatives? _____

- What does he normally wear when photographing a wedding? _____

- Will he wear a tuxedo or other specified attire? _____

- Ask if he is a member of Wedding Photographers International. Membership usually reflects a high level of professional competence and ethics. _____

PHOTO AND VIDEO CHECKLIST

Before the Ceremony

- ❏ Bride alone in dress
- ❏ Bride touching up makeup or adjusting veil
- ❏ Bride with mother
- ❏ Bride with maid or matron of honor
- ❏ Bride with bridesmaids
- ❏ Bride with both parents
- ❏ Bride putting on garter or placing penny in shoe
- ❏ Everyone getting their flowers
- ❏ Bride leaving house
- ❏ Bride and father getting into the car
- ❏ Groom alone
- ❏ Groom with best man, shaking hands, looking at his watch
- ❏ Groom and ushers putting on boutonnieres
- ❏ Groom with his parents
- ❏ Groom leaving for the ceremony
- ❏ Other moments dressing

Others
- ❏ _____
- ❏ _____
- ❏ _____

At the Ceremony

- ❏ Guests arriving
- ❏ Bride and father getting out of car
- ❏ Groom's parents being seated, or in procession
- ❏ Bride's mother being seated, or in procession

- ❏ Usher escorting guests
- ❏ Groom and groomsmen at the altar
- ❏ The processional
- ❏ Bride and father starting down the aisle
- ❏ The altar and decorations
- ❏ Giving-away ceremony
- ❏ Bride and groom exchanging vows
- ❏ Ring ceremony
- ❏ The kiss
- ❏ Bride and groom coming up the aisle
- ❏ The recessional
- ❏ Bride and groom outside place of worship with guests
- ❏ Bride and groom getting into the car
- ❏ Bride and groom looking through rear car window

Others
- ❏ _____
- ❏ _____
- ❏ _____

Before the Reception

- ❏ The couple together
- ❏ Bride with her attendants
- ❏ Groom with his attendants
- ❏ Bride and groom with all the attendants
- ❏ Bride and groom with their honor attendants
- ❏ Bride and groom with child attendants
- ❏ Bride with her parents
- ❏ Groom with his parents
- ❏ Both families together
- ❏ Bride and groom with officiant
- ❏ Bride's and groom's hands

Photography and Videography

Others

- ☐ _____
- ☐ _____
- ☐ _____

At the Reception

- ☐ Bride and groom getting out of the car
- ☐ Bride and groom making a grand entrance
- ☐ The receiving line
- ☐ The couple greeting guests in the receiving line
- ☐ Guests signing the guest book
- ☐ Bride and groom dancing
- ☐ Bride and her father dancing
- ☐ Groom dancing with his mother
- ☐ Bride dancing with her father-in-law
- ☐ Groom dancing with his mother-in-law
- ☐ Both sets of parents dancing
- ☐ Bridesmaids and ushers dancing
- ☐ Guests dancing
- ☐ The cake table
- ☐ Bride and groom cutting the cake
- ☐ The couple feeding cake to each other
- ☐ Bride and groom receiving toasts
- ☐ Buffet tables
- ☐ The bridal party's table
- ☐ The parents' table
- ☐ The guests' tables
- ☐ The musicians
- ☐ Bride tossing the bouquet
- ☐ Groom tossing the garter
- ☐ Bride and groom changing into going-away clothes

- ☐ Bride and groom saying good-by to parents
- ☐ Guests throwing rice
- ☐ Decorated getaway car
- ☐ Bride and groom getting into the car
- ☐ Guests waving good-bye
- ☐ The couple looking out rear window as car drives off

Others

- ☐ _____
- ☐ _____
- ☐ _____

Names of guests photographer shouldn't miss. (Have a relative or attendant responsible for pointing these people out to the photographer.)

- ☐ _____
- ☐ _____
- ☐ _____
- ☐ _____
- ☐ _____
- ☐ _____
- ☐ _____

VIDEOGRAPHY

Since the quality of recorders and video equipment has improved dramatically in recent years, video taping is much more sophisticated. So it should come as no surprise that video taping is becoming as traditional as still photographs.

Capturing your wedding on video tape can preserve a very precious memory for you and your groom to review, enjoy, and share with family and friends for many years to come.

TYPES OF WEDDING VIDEOS

There are various types and qualities of wedding videos, along with a wide range of prices. Your personal preference and your budget will determine the type of video perfect for you. Be sure to check rules and regulations your ceremony site may have with regard to videotaping.

The following list describes the main types of videos to consider:

- **Straight-shot Footage.** This type of video is shot with only one camera and starts at the beginning of your ceremony and runs straight through to the end of the reception with no interruptions or editing. Since there is no editing, and only one camera, it is the least expensive option. Most videographers can add a special touch by putting the couple's names and wedding date at the beginning of the tape. Others might add music. Ask if there is an additional fee for this.

- **Nostalgic Format.** This type of video can be as long and as nostalgic as you'd like to make it. Usually starts by showing photographs of the couple as children, then progresses to photos of romantic, fun times they have shared together, followed by scenes from the ceremony, reception, and sometimes ending with shots from the honeymoon. Still photos are shot with video tape, and can be edited into the tape at any point, creating the master tape. This format needs to be post-edited and requires more editing time. Therefore, it will generally be more expensive.

- **Wedding Documentary Format.** This type of video documents the day. The segments of the day's events tell a story similar to the way the events occurred on your special day. It may start with shots of the bride and groom getting ready, then progresses through the ceremony and reception, capturing spontaneous moments and interviews with family and friends, then ends as the bride and groom leave the reception. This video format is the most popular and

most commonly used, and can vary in price, according to the quality of the equipment and editing. More visually effective and better quality is obtained when two cameras are used, and the tapes are post-edited rather than edited in-camera.

FINDING A GOOD VIDEOGRAPHER

- **Recommendations from Friends.** View the video tapes of friends who have recently been married. If you are impressed with the quality of the tape, then get the name and number of that videographer.

- **Wedding Photographers.** Your wedding photographer can be one of the best sources, since photographers and videographers have to work together at weddings all the time. They should know several people in the industry, and will be able to give you names of a few they work with best. Still, set up appointments to view their sample tapes yourself; then book the one you like best.

- **Bridal Fairs.** Bridal fairs or local bridal shows are a great place to meet and see samples of videographers' work. Get cards and information about the ones that impressed you most; then follow up with a more in-depth interview.

- **Ceremony Site Coordinators.** Since many of the ceremony site coordinators go over the rules and regulations with the videographer and are there the day of the wedding to view his work, they can often be a good source. They will also recommend someone who is familiar with your ceremony location and its regulations.

- **Bridal Magazines.** Sometimes larger, established videography companies will run regional ads in the national bridal magazines. Still, interview them and view their sample tapes. You may even want to get a list of references.

WHAT MAKES A HIGH-QUALITY VIDEO

These are a few things to look for when viewing a sample tape of a videographer you're considering.

- All the equipment used must be the most up-to-date, high-quality, professional video equipment, including the editing and dubbing machine.

- Experienced videographers will look for spontaneous and natural reactions to record, while maintaining a formal approach to the ceremony.

- The segments of events in the video should tell a story, detailing the way the events occurred on your wedding day.

- Look for good, steady use of the camera, clear sound, good color and a sharp picture.

- Notice how the shots are framed. Does the image fill the frame nicely, without having certain things cut out, like the bride's headpiece?

- Notice the editing techniques used. Do they use a seamless electronic method of editing? Does the video look smooth as it moves from one scene to the next?

TYPES OF EDITING AND EQUIPMENT

EDITING

- **In-Camera Editing.** This type of editing is done while the tape is still in the camera. The videographer will simply stop shooting footage during uninteresting moments, or he can rewind the tape and shoot over unwanted footage. This editing format leaves little room for error, involves little or no post-editing, and is the least expensive way to go.

- **Post-Editing.** This type of editing is done after the ceremony and reception. The videographer reviews all the footage (many times footage from two cameras), then edits together the most interesting moments in the sequence of events, as they occurred that day. Music, special effects, titles and still photographs can also be dubbed or edited in to make the video look professional and of the same high quality that you would see on television.

MICROPHONES

- **Boom Microphones.** The boom microphone is the one you've often seen, which sticks up in the air and picks up every sound in the room. Besides being the least effective, it is also cumbersome, and not commonly used anymore.

- **Wired Microphones.** This method of obtaining sound is done through the use of a small microphone which has a wire that is connected to the camera. The microphone is usually clipped onto the groom, officiant or podium. The biggest problem with this type of microphone is that it limits your movement.

- **Wireless Microphones.** The small wireless microphone is probably the most popular means of picking up the audio on wedding videos today. The sound picked up by this small microphone is transmitted to the camera by a radio transmitter, usually worn around the groom's waist. To avoid picking up any outside interference and to get good clear sound, be sure the videographer uses a high band wireless microphone.

VIDEO CAMERAS

- **Consumer.** Consumer video cameras are the video cameras most often bought by the general public, and are for home use. Although equipment has been much improved, the tape quality is still not top-quality professional.

- **Professional.** Professional-grade video cameras are those that are most commonly used among professional videographers, those who do this as a serious business. Since these cameras use two computer chips, instead of the one used in consumer cameras, to process and separate colors, the picture you get is so much brighter and sharper. With new technology, these cameras have not only gotten better, but have become smaller and easier to maneuver. There is equipment available to shoot with VHS tape, or Super VHS tape, which is better quality and becoming more popular. Compact discs will be the next level of quality soon to be seen.

- **Commercial.** These commercial, or broadcast, quality cameras are the large, cumbersome cameras you see TV cameramen carry. These cameras require additional lighting; they are large, and they shoot 3/4 inch tape, rather than standard 1/2 inch VHS tape. Therefore, the 3/4 inch tape would have to be dubbed down to 1/2 inch tape so it could be played on your home video recorder. Even though the quality may be slightly better than using a professional grade camera, the cost will be more, and it is not a practical choice for a wedding.

TRENDS IN VIDEOGRAPHY

- **Videotaping Your Wedding.** The trend over the last few years is definitely toward having your wedding videotaped. About 80% of the couples today are choosing to have at least the ceremony, if not both the ceremony and reception, videotaped.

- **More Special Effects.** With the latest equipment and techniques available today, sophisticated videographers are using special effects and creative editing to produce wedding videos that have TV production quality. This slick production quality is definitely the trend; people are opting for this over videos that look like home movies, even though the price may be a little higher.

- **Still Photographs.** Another popular trend is to edit still photos into the video of the couple - as babies, or photos of special moments they have shared. Some are even ending the video with photos of their honeymoon.

- **High Quality.** The trend is toward high quality videos, shot with two cameras and post-edited with graphics, music and titles. High-band wireless microphones are used to capture good, clear sound, with ease of movement. The industry's technology is becoming more sophisticated, and so is the consumer.

FUN IDEAS

Have a friend videotape some of your pre-wedding shopping trips, and activities such as your shower and the rehearsal dinner. After documenting on video the preparations for your wedding, this tape can be edited together with your ceremony and reception tape, making a complete "documentary" of your wedding. To conclude the tape, consider adding some footage of your honeymoon. If the additional cost of this editing is not within your budget, or if you feel the quality of the pre-wedding tape does not come close to matching that of the wedding, then keep the pre-wedding tape as a separate memento.

WHAT TO ASK YOUR VIDEOGRAPHER

- Ask about the quality of the equipment and recording tapes they use. Is it updated, high-quality, professional video equipment, including editing and dubbing machines? _____

- How many cameras do they use to shoot the wedding? _____

- Do they use a wireless microphone, to capture the best audio? _____

- What type of editing do they do? Is it post-edited or in-camera edited? _____

- What is their fee? Is it an hourly charge or flat fee for shooting the wedding and reception? _____

- How many hours of coverage are provided? _____

- Are editing, titles and music included in the quoted price? _____

- Is the unedited master tape available to purchase? _____

- What is the cost of additional tapes? _____

- When will I receive my final tape? _____

- Are there any additional charges for mileage between wedding and reception? _____

- Are there any other charges that might be extra? _____

- Will they have back-up equipment in the event of a problem? _____

- Do they need any special lighting or electrical outlets? _____

- Are they familiar with your ceremony and reception locations? _____

- Have they shot a wedding in the location before? _____

- Will they meet you at the ceremony site ahead of time to go over the best shooting angles? _____

- Ask to see an actual video done by the person shooting your wedding. Sometimes large video companies show you samples done by the owner, then send someone less experienced to shoot your wedding. _____

- Ask to get a contract detailing exactly the type of video coverage you're expecting, number of cameras, amount and type of editing, titles and music included in the price, name of camera persons, the date, time, location and appropriate dress to be worn. _____

PHOTOGRAPHY WORKSHEET

	ESTIMATE #1		ESTIMATE #2	
	Name _____		Name _____	
	Phone _____		Phone _____	
	Description	**Cost**	**Description**	**Cost**
PORTRAITS Engagement Wedding				
PHOTOGRAPHER FEE Number of Hours Number of Shots				
WEDDING ALBUM Number of Pictures Size of Pictures				
PARENTS' ALBUM Number of Pictures Size of Pictures				
INDIVIDUAL PICTURES 8 x 10 5 x 7 4 x 5				
MISCELLANEOUS				
TOTAL				

PHOTOGRAPHER CHOICE

Name _____   Deposit _____

Address _____   Arrival Time _____

Phone _____   Date Ready/Balance Due _____

VIDEOGRAPHY WORKSHEET

	ESTIMATE #1 Name _____ Phone _____		**ESTIMATE #2** Name _____ Phone _____	
	Description	**Cost**	**Description**	**Cost**

VIDEOGRAPHER'S FEE
   Number of Hours
   Number of Cameras				

VIDEOTAPE LENGTH				
SOUND				
EDITING				
ADDITIONAL CASSETTES				
MISCELLANEOUS				
TOTAL				

VIDEOTAPE SERVICE CHOICE

Name _____   Deposit _____

Address _____   Arrival Time _____

Phone/Contact _____   Date Ready/Balance Due _____

PHOTOGRAPHER & VIDEOGRAPHER INFORMATION

Photocopy and provide a copy to the photographer and videographer.

Bride's name _____ Phone _____

Wedding Date _____ Time _____

Wedding Location _____

Reception Date _____ Time _____

Reception Location _____

PHOTOGRAPHER

Photographer _____ Phone _____

Assistant _____ Phone _____

Engagement Pictures: Date_____ Time_____

   Location _____

Bridal Portrait::   Date_____ Time_____

   Location _____

Wedding Day: Arrival time_____ Phone_____

   Location _____

Ceremony Site restrictions/guidelines _____

_____

_____

Appropriate dress _____

VIDEOGRAPHER

Videographer _____ Phone _____

Assistant _____ Phone _____

Wedding Day: Arrival time_____ Phone_____

   Location _____

Ceremony Site restrictions/guidelines _____

_____

_____

Appropriate dress _____

Wedding Transportation

rranging transportation is a very important step in planning a wedding, and something that should not be overlooked. After all, you want to make sure your wedding party, out-of-town guests, and most of all, the groom, arrive at the church and reception on time.

ARRANGING THE TRANSPORTATION

The key to this task is organization. It is the bride's responsibility to supply transportation, or at least arrange for it. First determine how many

people need transportation, where they need to be picked up and taken to. Depending on your budget, you may consider renting limousines for the entire wedding party, or at least one to take you and your father to the church, escort you and your groom to the reception, and for your final departure.

Limousines

Limousine service is available in most cities and can be found by looking in the local yellow pages. Call a few companies about a month before the ceremony to compare their prices. Be sure to ask the price per hour, the minimum number of hours (most require two to three hour minimums), and if there are any package rates. Most will require a credit card number or a deposit in advance to reserve the date, at which time the balance will be due.

When placing your reservation, you will have to give them the exact pick-up time, the address, the destination and approximate length of rental time needed. Be sure to ask about their cancellation policies.

If you find limousine service for the entire bridal party and out-of-town guests too costly, then arrange for friends or relatives to give a ride to those without their own transportation. You may also check into renting a large car or a van for their use. A nice touch is to send a car for the parents of the groom, if they don't live in your town.

Unique Modes of Transportation

Although you arrive at the church separately, you most definitely leave together – and that may be in any number of ways. Below is a list of ideas that others have tried.

• An antique car is a favorite; these may be rented, or possibly borrowed from a friend.

• Horsedrawn carriages are romantic, although they may be hard to find in your area.

• A hot air balloon is definitely a unique getaway.

• A fire engine has been used to take a couple from the church to the reception. Check with a local fire station.

• A horsedrawn sleigh could be a romantic touch for a winter wedding, or one at a ski resort.

• Pedicab – a cart for two which is pulled by a bicycle – is a novel mode of transportation, providing the distance is not too far.

• Boat or gondola, if the ceremony or reception is near water.

No matter how you leave, the important thing is that you are leaving as husband and wife, and on your way to a wonderful honeymoon.

DECORATING IDEAS FOR THE CAR

This tradition can be cute and fun, as long as it isn't damaging to the car, or hindering driving ability. Suggest that the decorators write "Just Married" on a large paper which can be taped to the back of the car, or suggest they use non-damaging paint. Do not let them use shaving cream, or, if they do, wash it off as soon as possible. Old shoes and tin cans along with colored streamers, ribbons, bows, bells and colorful balloons can make the car look festive.

Wedding Transportation

TRANSPORTATION WORKSHEET

OPTION #1

Name _____ Phone _____

Type of Vehicle _____ Cost per hour _____

Minimum hours _____ Overtime rate _____

OPTION #2

Name _____ Phone _____

Type of Vehicle _____ Cost per hour _____

Minimum hours _____ Overtime rate _____

OPTION #3

Name _____ Phone _____

Type of Vehicle _____ Cost per hour _____

Minimum hours _____ Overtime rate _____

COMPANY CONTRACTED WITH: Choice # _____

TRANSPORTATION NEEDS

Qty.	Description	# of Hours	Cost/Hour	Total Cost
_____	Limousines _____	_____	_____	_____
_____	Horsedrawn carriages _____	_____	_____	_____
_____	Horsedrawn sleighs _____	_____	_____	_____
_____	Antique cars _____	_____	_____	_____
_____	Rental cars _____	_____	_____	_____
_____	Trolley car/bus _____	_____	_____	_____
_____	Bus/van _____	_____	_____	_____
_____	Boat/gondola _____	_____	_____	_____
_____	Plane/helicopter _____	_____	_____	_____
_____	Hot-air balloon _____	_____	_____	_____
_____	Fire engine _____	_____	_____	_____
_____	Other _____	_____	_____	_____

Total Cost _____

Deposits Paid _____

Balance Due _____

WEDDING DAY TRANSPORTATION

TRANSPORTATION TO CEREMONY SITE

Name	Pick-up Time	Pick-up Location	Vehicle/Driver
Bride			
Bride's Father			
Bride's Mother			
Bridal Attendants			
Groom			
Groom's Attendants			
Groom's Parents			
Grandparents			
Other Guests			
_____			

TRANSPORTATION TO RECEPTION SITE

Name	Pick-up Time		Driver
Bride and Groom			
Bridal Attendants			
Groom's Attendants			
Bride's Parents			
Groom's Parents			
Grandparents			
Other Guests			
_____			

TRANSPORTATION FROM RECEPTION SITE TO HOTEL, HOME, ETC.

Name	Pick-up Time	Destination	Vehicle/Driver
Bride and Groom			
Bridal Attendants			
Groom's Attendants			
Bride's Parents			
Groom's Parents			
Grandparents			
Other Guests			
_____			

CHAPTER SIXTEEN

Pre-Wedding Parties

*T*he months before the wedding are always fun. Besides the excitement of being newly engaged and the planning and shopping, your friends and relatives will want to celebrate by honoring you with dinners and parties. Enjoy yourself while it lasts, but try not to schedule too many activities too close to the wedding. Show your appreciation with thank-you notes, or maybe a little gift or flowers to your host or hostess.

BRIDAL SHOWERS

Bridal showers are a time for your friends and family to meet and get to know one another before the wedding. The purpose of showers has always been to help outfit the couple's new home, or assemble the bride's trousseau. As tradition has it, a close friend, maid of honor, relative or bridesmaid may give you a shower. It is not proper for the shower to be hosted by your or your groom's mother or immediate family, although they may help.

Showers are usually given a month or two before the wedding. In order not to become a financial burden, it is better if two or three people host one together, rather than have several different showers. In the event you are given more than one, try not to invite the same people to every shower. Weddings can become expensive, especially for your bridal party, so don't take the joy out of it by sending them to the poor house.

Planning the Shower

Generally the hostess and the bride get together to determine a date, a guest list and the kind of shower it will be. Sometimes the hostess may surprise the bride and get the information from the fiancé. The traditional all- female shower is usually an afternoon luncheon or tea, with between ten and twenty guests. Invitations are usually sent, but they are not mandatory.

Not everyone who is invited to the wedding need be invited to the shower. Guests are usually close friends or relatives, or perhaps you may have one shower with each group. Avoid any hurt feelings by only inviting people to the shower who are invited to the reception, unless the wedding is taking place out of town, or only for close family members. A fun idea might be to have all the married women bring their wedding albums. It's fun to look back at your mother's, grandmother's, or a close friend's wedding.

Popular today, especially with older couples, are co-ed showers, which generally turn out to be just another party, but with gifts and, possibly, games. The men have a great time. When most of your friends are married, it is nice to plan the party for a weekend evening.

THEME SHOWERS

Theme showers are practical and very popular today. A theme is especially nice when there is

to be more than one shower. It can prevent duplicates.

Lingerie or Personal Showers

These showers are fun. Gifts can include all the beautiful things most people don't buy for themselves. They help prepare the trousseau for the honeymoon. Gifts may include lacy nightgowns, camisoles, sexy underwear, bras, or a nice robe. Other items may be perfume, bath accessories, or earrings. Or buy a pretty frame and get a baby picture of the bride's fiancé from his mother. It will not only surprise the bride, but will be something to cherish for years.

Linen Showers

These showers are always useful. You may want to let everyone know your color scheme. It can be helpful to register in a department store for items such as monogrammed towels, a scale, bathroom sets, sheets, pillows or a blanket.

Kitchen Showers

This is a great shower, especially if it's co-ed. Gift ideas are endless, and range from inexpensive to more expensive appliances. Browse through any kitchen store or department store again; it would be helpful if you were to register for items you need. One fun idea is to have each guest bring a favorite recipe along with one item needed for its preparation. Some examples: chocolate chip cookies with the cookie sheets, quiche lorraine with a quiche dish. The hostess may provide a recipe box to put the recipes in, or write them in a book designed for this, entitled "The Private Cookbook."

OPENING THE GIFTS

With all the excitement and passing of gifts, it's easy to misplace the cards. Have someone write down what the gift was and who it was given by, as soon as it's opened. She may want to jot down the first words out of your mouth; when reading back altogether at the end of the gift opening, it can be quite entertaining.

Make sure to show your appreciation by sending a thank-you note immediately. A unique thank-you note idea is to have the hostess take a picture of you and each guest as you open the gift; then surprise them with a photo thank-you card. These can be purchased through Kodak. They are like the Christmas cards, but without the message.

For more great ideas on shower themes, games, decorations, recipes and party favors, my latest book, "Showers," is an in-depth look at hosting a bridal shower that will be fun and memorable.

BRIDESMAIDS' PARTY

Throughout the pre-wedding months, your bridesmaids will probably have entertained you and been a big help with planning and shopping. It is a nice gesture for you to treat them to either a traditional luncheon, afternoon tea, or even a dinner party including their spouses or dates. Whichever you decide, it's a nice way to thank them, let them meet out-of-town attendants, take care of final dress fittings, and go over last minute plans. You may also decide to give them their gifts at that time.

THE BACHELOR PARTY

The bachelor party is very much a part of the wedding tradition. It is the groom's last night out with the boys as a single man. However, the custom is optional and may be hosted by the groom himself, his best man, or the ushers. The groom may also want to pass out his attendants' gifts or review their duties and last minute plans.

It's not a bad idea to see to it that the party is a few days or a week before the wedding. It traditionally starts with a dinner where the groom makes a champagne toast to his bride. After drinking to the toast, each of the men would smash his glass so that it could never be used for a less worthy purpose. The tradition is rarely carried to this extreme, but the groom may still toast his bride.

A WEDDING BRUNCH OR BREAKFAST

Hosting a light breakfast or early lunch is a great way for a friend or relative to participate in the wedding festivities, as long as it is not scheduled too near to the time of the wedding. If the wedding is late in the afternoon or evening, it will entertain your out-of-town guests while you take care of last-minute wedding-day preparations. Neither your family nor the groom's family is expected to attend. However, members may participate if time permits.

SHOWER GUEST AND GIFT LIST

Hostess(es) _____   Shower Date _____

Location _____   Time _____

Phone _____   Theme _____

RSVP Yes No	Guest's Name & Address	Gift	Thank you Sent
❏ ❏	_____	_____	____
❏ ❏	_____	_____	____
❏ ❏	_____	_____	____
❏ ❏	_____	_____	____
❏ ❏	_____	_____	____
❏ ❏	_____	_____	____
❏ ❏	_____	_____	____
❏ ❏	_____	_____	____
❏ ❏	_____	_____	____
❏ ❏	_____	_____	____
❏ ❏	_____	_____	____
❏ ❏	_____	_____	____
❏ ❏	_____	_____	____
❏ ❏	_____	_____	____
❏ ❏	_____	_____	____
❏ ❏	_____	_____	____
❏ ❏	_____	_____	____
❏ ❏	_____	_____	____
❏ ❏	_____	_____	____
❏ ❏	_____	_____	____
❏ ❏	_____	_____	____
❏ ❏	_____	_____	____
❏ ❏	_____	_____	____
❏ ❏	_____	_____	____
❏ ❏	_____	_____	____
❏ ❏	_____	_____	____
❏ ❏	_____	_____	____

BRIDAL LUNCHEON GUEST LIST

Luncheon site _____ Date _____ Time _____

Address _____ Number of guests _____

Contact person _____ Phone _____

RSVP			
Yes	No	*Name & Address*	*Phone*
❑	❑	_____	_____
❑	❑	_____	_____
❑	❑	_____	_____
❑	❑	_____	_____
❑	❑	_____	_____
❑	❑	_____	_____
❑	❑	_____	_____
❑	❑	_____	_____
❑	❑	_____	_____
❑	❑	_____	_____
❑	❑	_____	_____
❑	❑	_____	_____
❑	❑	_____	_____
❑	❑	_____	_____
❑	❑	_____	_____
❑	❑	_____	_____
❑	❑	_____	_____
❑	❑	_____	_____
❑	❑	_____	_____
❑	❑	_____	_____
❑	❑	_____	_____
❑	❑	_____	_____
❑	❑	_____	_____
❑	❑	_____	_____
❑	❑	_____	_____
❑	❑	_____	_____

BRIDAL LUNCHEON WORKSHEET

OPTION #1

Name _____ Date _____ Time _____

Address _____

Contact person _____ Phone _____

Menu Items	Cost	Decorations, linens, etc.	Cost
_____	___	_____	___
_____	___	_____	___
_____	___	_____	___
_____	___	_____	___

Gratuity included: Yes ❑   No ❑   **Estimated cost per person** _____

OPTION #2

Name _____ Date _____ Time _____

Address _____

Contact person _____ Phone _____

Menu Items	Cost	Decorations, linens, etc.	Cost
_____	___	_____	___
_____	___	_____	___
_____	___	_____	___
_____	___	_____	___

Gratuity included: Yes ❑   No ❑   **Estimated cost per person** _____

FINAL CHOICE: #_____   Date Scheduled _____ Time _____

Final Menu Items	Cost	Decorations, linens, etc.	Cost
Appetizer: _____	___	_____	___
Soup/Salad: _____	___	_____	___
Entrée: _____	___	_____	___
Dessert: _____	___	Flowers: _____	___
Beverage: _____	___	Party Favors: _____	___
Other: _____	___	Other: _____	___

Total cost _____ **Deposit paid** _____ **Balance due** _____

Activities and notes: _____

_____

WEDDING BRUNCH WORKSHEET

Hostess/Site _____ Date _____ Time _____

Address _____ Number of guests _____

Contact person _____ Phone _____

GUEST LIST

RSVP Yes No	Name & Address	Phone
❑ ❑	_____	_____
❑ ❑	_____	_____
❑ ❑	_____	_____
❑ ❑	_____	_____
❑ ❑	_____	_____
❑ ❑	_____	_____
❑ ❑	_____	_____
❑ ❑	_____	_____
❑ ❑	_____	_____
❑ ❑	_____	_____
❑ ❑	_____	_____
❑ ❑	_____	_____
❑ ❑	_____	_____
❑ ❑	_____	_____
❑ ❑	_____	_____
❑ ❑	_____	_____

BRUNCH DETAILS

Menu & Beverages	Cost	Decorations, Rentals, etc.	Cost
_____	_____	_____	_____
_____	_____	_____	_____
_____	_____	_____	_____
_____	_____	_____	_____
_____	_____	_____	_____

Activities and notes: _____

PRE-WEDDING PARTY WORKSHEET

Type of party _____   Date _____   Time _____

Hostess/Site _____   Phone _____

Address _____   Number of guests _____

GUEST LIST

RSVP Yes No	Name & Address	Phone
❏ ❏	_____	_____
❏ ❏	_____	_____
❏ ❏	_____	_____
❏ ❏	_____	_____
❏ ❏	_____	_____
❏ ❏	_____	_____
❏ ❏	_____	_____
❏ ❏	_____	_____
❏ ❏	_____	_____
❏ ❏	_____	_____
❏ ❏	_____	_____
❏ ❏	_____	_____
❏ ❏	_____	_____
❏ ❏	_____	_____
❏ ❏	_____	_____
❏ ❏	_____	_____

PARTY DETAILS

Menu & Beverages	Cost	Decorations, Rentals, etc.	Cost
_____	_____	_____	_____
_____	_____	_____	_____
_____	_____	_____	_____
_____	_____	_____	_____

Activities and notes: _____

CHAPTER SEVENTEEN

Wedding Gifts

Bridal gift registries are a big help to everyone, so don't hesitate to use them. With the price of gifts today and the expense of setting up a new home, a gift-giver can feel the money is being spent on something you need and want. It is also a tremendous help to you when trying to complete your china, silver and crystal service. It specifies your pattern and what pieces you still need. It helps to prevent duplicates and avoid exchanges.

GIFT REGISTRIES

Most fine china and department stores have free bridal registries. Today many stores use computers so the registry information may be obtained at any one of their locations. This is a big help if you have friends or relatives in other cities. You may consider registering at more than one store. To avoid duplication it is best to register for different things at each store, or to divide the number needed between the stores. If your registration does overlap in some areas, be sure to update the stores as gifts arrive.

When and What to Register For

Start shopping early to allow yourself plenty of time to make these decisions. They will be with you a long time – so don't choose with haste. With the many decisions to make and choices available, get organized before you start. Use the shopping list provided to determine what items you need. If you have both been living on your own, there are probably a lot of kitchen items you already have. You certainly don't need three toasters. Take your checklist and start window shopping. If your fiancé hates to shop, you can narrow down the choices and bring him along to make the final decisions.

The registry consultant can be a big help, so don't hesitate to ask about kitchenware demonstrations, fashion shows, or special sales coming up. Register for items in several different price ranges. Smaller, less expensive items make good shower gifts and large, more expensive items may be purchased by a few friends together. Once your final choices have been made, let both families and friends know so they can spread the word.

The gift registry checklist will help you keep track of your wedding gifts. Take this list with you when you go shopping. Write down the name of the store where each item is registered and mark the number of items you want. Once gifts are received, update the number in the "rec'd" box.

DISPLAYING GIFTS

Today people are getting away from the practice of displaying gifts. Many feel it is not in good taste. The true meaning of a gift is a personal expression of love and it should not be judged or viewed for its monetary value. This does not mean to say that you won't be excited and want family and close friends to see the beautiful gifts.

Other people choose to follow the old tradition and display gifts, with the donor's name, at the home of the bride or her parents. The gifts are grouped in categories. For gifts of more than one set, such as china, only display one place setting, not each one received. Do not place extravagant gifts next to modest ones, or display monetary gifts. Avoid the possibility of embarrassing anyone.

Gifts at the Reception

Even though most guests will probably send their gift directly to your home, some guests will inevitably bring the gift to the reception. Set aside a specific table for gifts in an area that will be safe, and not in the way. See if the gifts can be taken to a closet or locked room, since, unfortunately, gifts have been known to "walk away" from receptions, and certainly the person in charge of them will not want to spend the entire reception guarding them.

Another reminder: Give the person in charge of the gifts some scotch tape to secure the cards to each gift immediately. This will prevent confusion later. Gifts should not be opened at the reception, but can be opened later that evening or on the following day.

Gifts Without Cards

Occasionally gifts are received that do not bear gift cards. If it looks as though the gift was sent from a store, contact the store to try to track down the giver. Many stores write a code inside the box that designates the store location, date of purchase and sales person – all of which information can be helpful in figuring out who might have sent the gift.

Wedding Gifts

If the gift was brought to the reception, you have a real problem on your hands. First, you can eliminate as the mystery giver all those guests whose gifts you have already received. If there is only one gift and one guest unaccounted for, you're in luck. They will probably match up. Chances are, however, that won't be the case. You may well have several gifts without cards. It's time then to use the process of elimination. As gifts continue to arrive (and there will be plenty of late ones – guests have up to one year to send you a gift, unfortunately), you may eliminate those late givers from the mystery. Eventually, you should narrow it down to the unknown giver. If you still have a gift, or gifts, unaccounted for, you may need friends or family members to try to find out discreetly what those guests you haven't heard from gave you. It is inappropriate for you to ask guests yourself.

RETURNING AND EXCHANGING GIFTS

If you receive duplicate or inappropriate gifts, make sure to keep the box or tags that came with them. Most stores are cooperative with returns, or will at least exchange a gift for something else. Send a thank-you note immediately for the gift. It is best not to mention the return or exchange.

When gifts arrive damaged, it is best to notify the store first, rather than the sender. You may even want to take a picture if the box is damaged. Generally there will be no problem with replacing it.

SENDING THANK-YOU NOTES

- Every gift you receive should be followed by a thank-you note, even if you have thanked the giver in person.

- It is appropriate to send a thank-you note as soon as possible. The note should be sent within two weeks for gifts received before the wedding, and one month for those received at the wedding or later.

- It's best to keep up with thank-you notes as gifts are received, so you aren't totally buried in owed correspondence. A printed card letting the giver know the gift has been received can be sent if you are too busy, or have a large number of gifts to acknowledge. This card should be followed as soon as possible by a hand-written note.

- Your thank-you notes should always be signed with your maiden name if sent before the wedding, and your married name after the wedding (unless you are keeping your maiden name).

- Most thank-you notes are written by the bride. They can be signed by the couple, or may be signed only by the bride when she has mentioned her groom's name in the note.

- When thanking a married couple, address the note to both of them. You may address the note only to the wife, if you also refer to her husband in the body of the note.

- There is nothing that says thank-you notes must be written only by the bride, so enlist the help of your groom. Have him write notes to his family members or close friends.

- When a joint gift is given by your bridesmaids, an individual note to each, expressing your thanks, should be sent. However, if a joint gift is given by a large group of employees or club members, one thank-you note addressed to the group would be appropriate.

TIPS ON WRITING THANK-YOU NOTES

- Address the thank-you note to the giver, starting with *"Dear . . . ."* The note can be addressed to both husband and wife, or addressed only to the wife, when the husband's name is mentioned in the body of the note.

- When the gift is from a group of four or more people (except your bridesmaids), such as a group of co-workers, address them together: *"Dear Friends."*

- Begin your note by thanking the giver and mentioning what the gift is. *"Thank you so much for the lovely crystal vase you and Mr. Jones sent."*

  In the second sentence, mention how you and your husband (use his name) will use the gift. *"John and I love fresh flowers – your vase filled with them will look beautiful in our new home."* When the gift is money, be sure to tell the giver what you will be using it for.

- Third or fourth sentences should add a personal thought; it can be almost anything, depending on how well you know the giver. *"We're so pleased that you are able to attend our wedding – we both look forward to seeing you"* or *"I'm glad you are able to be at our wedding – I look forward to meeting you."*

- Close the note by thanking the giver again. *"Thank you again."* or *"Again, many thanks."*

- Sign the note with your maiden name before the wedding and your married name after (unless you keep your maiden name.) Use both your first and last names, especially when you don't know the giver well. Just above your name sign off with: *"Sincerely," "Love," "With much love," "Fondly,"* or whatever you feel is appropriate, given how well you know them.

GIFT REGISTRY CHECKLIST

FORMAL DINNERWARE	Wants	Rec'd
Store:		
Phone:		
Pattern:		
Manufacturer:		
Dinner plate		
Luncheon plate		
Dessert/salad plate		
Bread/butter plate		
Buffet plate		
Cream soup bowl		
Soup/cereal bowl		
Fruit bowl		
Rim soup bowl		
Coffee cup/saucer		
Demitasse/saucer		
Teacup/saucer		
Teapot		
Coffeepot		
Sugar/creamer		
Salt/pepper		
Serving bowls		
Serving platters		
Gravy boat		
Egg cup		
Other:		

INFORMAL DINNERWARE	Wants	Rec'd
Store:		
Phone:		
Pattern:		
Manufacturer:		
Dinner plate		
Salad plate		
Bowls		
Cups/saucers		
Mugs		
Serving pieces		
Other:		

FORMAL FLATWARE	Wants	Rec'd
Store:		
Phone:		
Pattern:		
Manufacturer:		
Dinner fork		
Dessert/salad fork		
Cocktail fork		
Tablespoon		
Soup spoon		
Tea/dessert spoon		
Demitasse spoon		
Ice tea spoon		
Dinner knife		
Steak knife		
Butter spreader		
Serving spoon		
Gravy ladle		
Serving fork		
Cold meat fork		
Cake knife		
Pie server		
Salad set		
Carving set		
Sugar spoon/tongs		
Lemon fork		
Butter knife		
Silver chest		
Other:		

INFORMAL FLATWARE	Wants	Rec'd
Store:		
Phone:		
Pattern:		
Manufacturer:		
No. of place settings		
Serving pieces		
Other:		

HOLLOWARE/SERVERS	Wants	Rec'd
Tea service		
Coffee service		
Water pitcher		
Champagne cooler		
Serving bowls		
Serving platters		
Trays		
Bread tray		
Service plates		
Salad bowl		
Compote		
Tureen		
Chafing dish		
Condiment dish		
Cream/sugar set		
Salt/pepper		
Dessert dishes		
Gravy boat		
Candlesticks		
Napkin rings		
Other:		

CRYSTAL	Wants	Rec'd
Store:		
Phone:		
Pattern:		
Manufacturer:		
Goblets		
White wine		
Claret		
Champagne		
Liqueur		
Brandy		
Cocktail		
Iced tea		
Other:		

GIFT REGISTRY CHECKLIST

CASUAL GLASS/BARWARE	Wants	Rec'd
Store:		
Phone:		
Pattern:		
Manufacturer:		
Goblets		
Wine		
Old-fashioned		
Highball		
Iced tea		
Beer mugs		
Cocktail		
Fruit juice		
Other:		

BAR NEEDS	Wants	Rec'd
Ice bucket		
Wine rack		
Ice crusher		
Coasters		
Jigger/tools		
Corkscrew/wine opener		
Punch bowl set		
Decanters		
Other:		

KITCHENWARE	Wants	Rec'd
Coffee maker		
Coffee grinder		
Juicer		
Food processor		
Blender		
Mixer		
Microwave		
Toaster/toaster oven		
Electric skillet		
Deep fryer		
Slow cooker		
Pressure cooker		

	Wants	Rec'd
Microwave cookware		
Ovenware		
Cookware		
Bakeware		
Wok		
Tea kettle		
Hot tray		
Mixing bowls		
Storage containers		
Cannister set		
Spice rack		
Kitchen utensils		
Cutlery		
Cutting board		
Wooden Salad bowl set		
Other:		

LINENS	Wants	Rec'd
Formal cloth/napkins		
Informal cloth/napkins		
Place mats		
Cocktail napkins		
Potholders/dish towels		
Aprons		
Comforter		
Bedspread		
Mattress pad		
Pillows		
Bed sheets		
Blanket		
Electric blanket		
Beach towels		
Bath towels/face cloths		
Guest towels		
Bath mat		
Rug/lid cover set		
Accessories		
Other:		

DECORATIVE ITEMS	Wants	Rec'd
Vases		
Lamps		
Clocks		
Pictures		
Bookends		
Area rugs		
Baskets		
TV tables		
Accessories		
Other:		

ELECTRONICS	Wants	Rec'd
TV/video system		
Stereo		
Camera equipment		
Clock radio		
Portable TV/radio		
Calculator		
Security devices		
Telephones		
Other:		

GENERAL	Wants	Rec'd
Luggage:		
Exercise/sporting equip.		
Barbecue		
Patio Furniture		
Picnic basket		
Sleeping bags		
Carpet cleaner		
Tools		
Hobbies/games		
Others:		

GIFT LIST

Name	Gift	Store	Thank-you Sent
1.			
2.			
3.			
4.			
5.			
6.			
7.			
8.			
9.			
10.			
11.			
12.			
13.			
14.			
15.			
16.			
17.			
18.			
19.			
20.			
21.			
22.			
23.			
24.			
25.			
26.			
27.			
28.			
29.			
30.			
31.			
32.			
33.			

GIFT LIST

	Name	Gift	Store	Thank-you Sent
34.				
35.				
36.				
37.				
38.				
39.				
40.				
41.				
42.				
43.				
44.				
45.				
46.				
47.				
48.				
49.				
50.				
51.				
52.				
53.				
54.				
55.				
56.				
57.				
58.				
59.				
60.				
61.				
62.				
63.				
64.				
65.				
66.				

GIFT LIST

	Name	Gift	Store	Thank-you Sent
67.				
68.				
69.				
70.				
71.				
72.				
73.				
74.				
75.				
76.				
77.				
78.				
79.				
80.				
81.				
82.				
83.				
84.				
85.				
86.				
87.				
88.				
89.				
90.				
91.				
92.				
93.				
94.				
95.				
96.				
97.				
98.				
99.				

GIFT LIST

	Name	Gift	Store	Thank-you Sent
100.				
101.				
102.				
103.				
104.				
105.				
106.				
107.				
108.				
109.				
110.				
111.				
112.				
113.				
114.				
115.				
116.				
117.				
118.				
119.				
120.				
121.				
122.				
123.				
124.				
125.				
126.				
127.				
128.				
129.				
130.				
131.				
132.				

GIFT LIST

	Name	Gift	Store	Thank-you Sent
133.				
134.				
135.				
136.				
137.				
138.				
139.				
140.				
141.				
142.				
143.				
144.				
145.				
146.				
147.				
148.				
149.				
150.				
151.				
152.				
153.				
154.				
155.				
156.				
157.				
158.				
159.				
160.				
161.				
162.				
163.				
164.				
165.				

GIFT LIST

Name	Gift	Store	Thank-you Sent
166.			
167.			
168.			
169.			
170.			
171.			
172.			
173.			
174.			
175.			
176.			
177.			
178.			
179.			
180.			
181.			
182.			
183.			
184.			
185.			
186.			
187.			
188.			
189.			
190.			
191.			
192.			
193.			
194.			
195.			
196.			
197.			
198.			

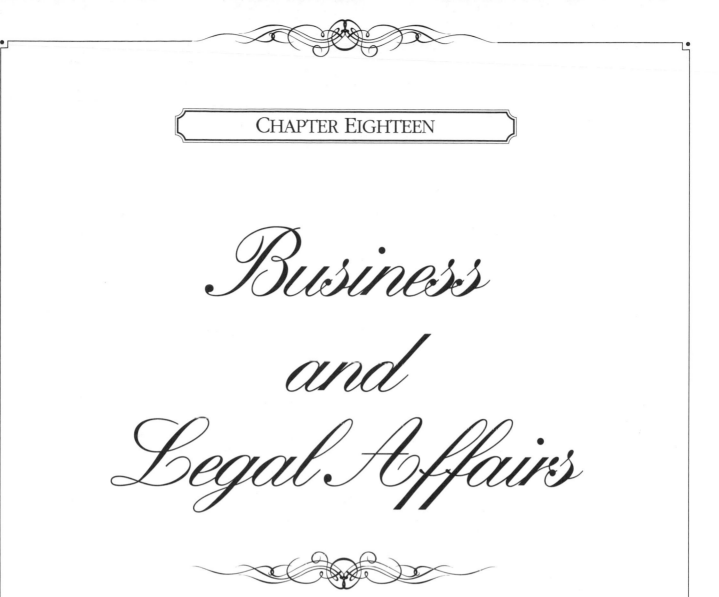

CHAPTER EIGHTEEN

Business and Legal Affairs

here are certain business and legal affairs you should think about and take care of before your wedding. These include getting contracts from people who will be supplying your wedding needs, getting your marriage license, changing your name if you plan to, and preparing a prenuptial agreement if you are signing one.

YOUR MARRIAGE LICENSE

Marriage license requirements are determined by each state. Those requirements may be obtained by calling or writing the County Clerk's office. The requirements may vary from state to state, but generally they are laws concerned with the age of consent, residence, citizenship requirements, and freedom of couples from venereal disease.

Things to find out and what to take:

- Do you need to apply in person and together?

- What is the waiting time before and after the license is issued?

- Who needs to sign it?

- What age requirements apply to the bride and groom?

- What are the residence requirements?

- Is a blood test or doctor's certificate needed?

- What is the fee?

- What identification or proof of age is required?

- Is proof of divorce needed?

- Are AID's tests required? If so, have the test done about three months in advance. It can take six to eight weeks to get the results back.

TO CHANGE YOUR NAME, OR NOT?

As a bride today, you have a lot of options. Consider your particular situation and determine which option fits your need and preference. Will it be to keep your maiden name, take your husband's last name, hyphenate both names, or use yours as a middle name? Even though over the years most women have taken their husband's last name, it is not legally required that you do so.

More and more women today are choosing to keep or incorporate their own last name. But many are sticking with tradition and taking their husband's names. Decisions are based on a variety of reasons, among them: professional status, ease of spelling and pronunciation, desire to keep your family name, feeling of commitment and tradition, for children's sake, or for social ease.

You must determine which name you will use legally and then which name you will use socially. The following are a few options and what is required to exercise them.

- **Keep Your Maiden Name.** Should you choose to keep your maiden name, in most states you don't have to notify any official agencies. Check your state for any special requirements. Sign your maiden name on the marriage certificate and on all legal documents just as you did before.

- **Use Your Maiden Name Professionally, and Your Husband's Name Socially.** Many women are choosing this option, especially when they are already established and known professionally by their maiden names. Problems can arise when you intermix the two names on legal documents. To avoid this, use only your maiden name on all legal documents and when filing your joint tax return. The IRS may require proof of your marriage and request a notarized copy of your marriage license.

- **Hyphenate Your Names.** This is a popular option when you want to retain both last names. The woman's last name appears first, followed by the husband's last name. The woman may decide to use the full hyphenated name on legal documents, and use only her husband's last name socially.

  Be sure to record your name change with all the agencies listed on the "Name and Address Change Worksheet," and sign your marriage certificate the same way.

- **Taking Your Husband's Name.** If you are planning to change your name by taking, or adding, your husband's last name, start by signing that name on the marriage certificate and all future documents. Get the necessary paper work or requirements to record your name change on all legal and official records.

- **Have Your Husband Take Your Name.** It's not a common practice, but today some grooms are changing to their wife's last name. This is a viable alternative when the wife, for professional reasons, can't change her last name, and the couple wants to use just one name for family and social ease. Another reason might be if the groom's name is difficult to spell and pronounce. He should make the same changes on legal and official records that are listed on the "Name and Address Change Worksheet" and contact the local County Clerk's office to see if there are any further requirements in your state.

CHANGING YOUR NAME AND ADDRESS

If you are planning on changing your name, you may want to take care of some changes before the wedding. Some may require a copy of your marriage license with notification, so check ahead of time.

- Social Security card - local office of the Federal Social Security Administration.
- Driver's license
- Car registration
- Voter's registration
- Passport
- Employer or school records
- Bank accounts – changing or opening joint accounts
- Stocks or bonds
- Wills – drawing up a will or changing the beneficiary
- Insurance policies – automobiles, home, health
- Pension plans

- Property titles or leases
- Charge accounts
- Subscriptions
- Club memberships
- Post Office – new name and new address

PRENUPTIAL AGREEMENTS

Today more and more couples are marrying later in life and they have accumulated assets, or have established careers, before getting married. Others are marrying for the second or third time and have assets from previous marriages, children's support, or inheritance to consider. Many of these couples are turning to the use of prenuptial agreements to clarify what each person brings into the marriage, and how the assets will be split in the event of a divorce or death.

The Prenuptial Agreement

The prenuptial agreement is a legal contract entered into before the marriage (a postnuptial agreement is entered into after the marriage). This contract is designed to anticipate and resolve areas that could become a matter of dispute between the two parties at a later date. Prenuptial agreements are most commonly used in pre-arranging financial matters and protecting future inheritances. But they may also be used to specify rights and privileges within a marriage, or to provide for the division of property, or the custody of children in the case of divorce. The terms of the agreement become legally enforceable only when the parties are seeking a divorce or when one of them dies.

Who Needs a Prenuptial Agreement

If you are both very young, have not accumulated any real assets, and are not likely to inherit a sizable amount, you probably don't need a prenuptial agreement. Each state has laws that automatically establish certain contractual regulations on how property is divided. Once you are husband and wife, these existing laws may fit your needs perfectly well and no other contract would be necessary.

A prenuptial agreement should be considered by any individual, regardless of age or previous marital status, who is coming into the marriage with considerable assets, including stocks, real estate investments, cars, jewelry, art, or right of inheritance. Today most couples in this situation find nothing unromantic about planning their lives together in a practical way, especially when they both have such assets. Couples find the discussion and resolution of these issues will give them added security and more confidence in their decision to marry and build a life together.

The signing of a prenuptial agreement, or not, finally comes down to a decision you both will have to make. Discuss it openly and determine what's right for you. Some couples feel that discussing these matters and requesting a prenuptial agreement from your fiancé hinders the romance and shows a lack of commitment toward the marriage. Others feel the communication strengthens the trust and starts the marriage off on the right foot. The issue of prenuptial agreements deserves some serious consideration; you may find it helpful to consult a financial planner or an attorney to get some advice.

What To Do First

- Discuss important marital issues that you might want included in an agreement, especially assets, finances, children from previous marriages, and rights of inheritance.

- Consult a financial planner or attorney for advise. Have your agreements written in a legal contract drawn up by one or both of your attorneys.

- In your contract specify a certain time or date by which you will review or revise your contract if needed – every two to five years, for example. The contracts need not be cast in concrete.

What to Include

- All assets and property owned separately or jointly.

- How assets and liabilities will be handled in the event of a divorce.

- List, specifically, checking and savings accounts, credit cards, loans, cars, jewelry, art, real estate and other property.

- How right of inheritance will be handled (optional).

- How new assets will be divided.

- Who keeps the house or leased apartment, and how equity or deposits are divided.

- How future income will be shared. (If one spouse has put the other through law school, for example, that person will want a share of the law practice, even after a divorce.)

MARRIAGE LICENSE CHECKLIST

COUNTY CLERK'S OFFICE _____ Phone _____

Address _____

Appointment date _____ Time _____

State's minimum age to marry _____

Waiting period after application _____

License is valid for _____ days

License fee _____

BRIDE'S DOCTOR _____ Phone _____

Address _____

Appointment date _____ Exam fee _____

Need to get:

GROOM'S DOCTOR _____ Phone _____

Address _____

Appointment date _____ Exam fee _____

Documents and tests required by County Clerk in your state:

Required	Item	Have	*Need to get:* Bride/	Groom
_____	Proof of age (driver's license)	❑	❑	❑
_____	Proof of citizenship (birth certificate)	❑	❑	❑
_____	Doctor's certificate	❑	❑	❑
_____	Venereal disease blood test	❑	❑	❑
_____	Rubella, sickle cell anemia blood test	❑	❑	❑
_____	AIDS or other blood test	❑	❑	❑
_____	AIDS counseling	❑	❑	❑
_____	Proof of divorce	❑	❑	❑
_____	Parental consent for marriage of minors	❑	❑	❑

BRIDE'S NAME AND ADDRESS CHANGE WORKSHEET

Items to be Changed	Change Name	Change Address	Account or Policy Number, Other Information	Phone or Address To Notify Company	Done
Social Security					
Driver's license					
Car registration					
Voter's registration					
Passport					
Employee records					
School records					
Checking accounts					
Savings accounts					
IRA accounts					
Safety deposit box					
Stocks and bonds					
Loans					
Wills/trusts					
Pensions					
Property titles					
Leases					
Subscriptions					
Club memberships					
Post Office					
Auto insurance					
Property insurance					
Medical insurance					
Life Insurance					
Doctors/dentist					
Business Cards					
Business stationery					
Utilities					
Taxes					
Credit Cards:					

GROOM'S CHANGE OF ADDRESS & MARITAL STATUS WORKSHEET

Items to be Changed	Change Marital Status	Change Address	Account or Policy Number, Other Information	Phone or Address To Notify Company	Done
Social Security					
Driver's license					
Car registration					
Voter's registration					
Passport					
Employee records					
School records					
Checking accounts					
Savings accounts					
IRA accounts					
Safety deposit box					
Stocks and bonds					
Loans					
Wills/trusts					
Pensions					
Property titles					
Leases					
Subscriptions					
Club memberships					
Post Office					
Life insurance					
Auto insurance					
Property insurance					
Medical insurance					
Utilities					
Doctors/dentist					
Business stationery					
Taxes					
Credit Cards:					

NAME AND ADDRESS CHANGE FORM LETTER

To Whom it may Concern:

This letter is to inform you of our recent marriage and our change of address.

The account/policy number to be changed is: _____

Currently under the name of: _____

Social Security Number (where applicable) _____

PREVIOUS INFORMATION

_____
Husband's name

_____
Husband's previous address

_____
City   *State*   *Zip*
(   ) _____
Phone

_____
Wife's maiden name

_____
Wife's previous address

_____
City   *State*   *Zip*
(   ) _____
Phone

NEW INFORMATION

_____
Husband's full name

_____
Wife's full name

_____
New address

_____
City   *State*   *Zip*

_____
Social Security Number (when applicable)

_____
Social Security Number (when applicable)

(   ) _____
Phone

As of this date _____ please change the following:

❏ Change name   ❏ Change address & phone   ❏ Add spouse's name

Special Instructions: _____

_____

_____

Please send any additional forms or requirements to facilitate these changes.
If you have any questions, please contact us!

Sincerely,

Husband's signature _____

Wife's signature _____

CHAPTER NINETEEN

Second Marriages and Reaffirmations

With second marriages amounting to thirty percent of all marriages today, many of the old traditions are changing. There are a number of alternatives and choices that may fit your individual situation. Your decisions may be determined by you and your fiancé's age, whether children are involved, and if this is a second marriage for both of you or just one of you. The following information is to help you consider your options so you can choose the kind of ceremony and reception that will make you feel good.

ANNOUNCING YOUR ENGAGEMENT

When children from previous marriages are involved, it is best to tell them first. Chances are they already have an idea, but they still should hear the news from you. Make sure it is handled carefully and with love. You want them to feel they are gaining a parent, not threatened by the thought of losing one. It is proper to notify a former spouse when children are involved.

Afterwards, let your parents know the good news; then, of course, tell your friends and relatives. Traditionally, if it is the bride's second marriage, a formal announcement is not made. If it is the bride's first, and the groom's second, marriage, a formal engagement announcement is customary.

PLANNING YOUR CEREMONY

When it is the bride's first marriage and the groom's second, generally everything remains traditional. The wedding may be as formal and religious as you would like, depending on your particular denomination.

One of the first things you should do in planning a second wedding is meet with the clergyman or official you would like to perform the ceremony. Find out all regulations or restrictions on the remarriage of a divorced person.

Traditionally, when it is the bride's second marriage, a semiformal or informal wedding is chosen, rather than a large, very formal wedding. Only close friends and family members are present. The exception to this could be if the bride never had a large, formal first wedding, or has no children. Another exception could be when it is the bride's second, but the groom's first, marriage. In this case the groom's parents may want to host the wedding or the couple may choose to pay for it themselves. In any case, it is not right to expect the bride's family to pay for a second large wedding.

When it is both the bride's and groom's second marriage, it is best to have a tasteful semiformal or informal wedding. It may still be in a church, chapel, home, hotel or club. There should be a maid or matron of honor in the ceremony but no bridesmaids. Similarly, the groom should have a best man but should only have ushers if they are needed. Ushers that are needed do not stand at the altar. When there are children from previous marriages, the couple may want to involve them in some way, depending on their ages.

THE WEDDING DRESS

With the increase of second marriages, designers in the bridal industry are making a great number of beautiful dresses for the second-time bride-to-be. You may select a romantically feminine, lacy dress of mid-calf or ankle length in white or ivory, or a traditionally elegant knee length dress or suit in white or pastel. What you choose to wear will depend on the formality of the ceremony, the time of day and, most important, what you feel good wearing.

Yes, you may wear white. However, a veil, the symbol of virginity, should not be worn. Instead, wear a hat or a wreath of fresh flowers. You may also want to carry a bouquet or a flower-trimmed prayer book.

INVITATIONS AND ANNOUNCEMENTS

When the ceremony is larger than just a few close friends and relatives, including, say, thirty or more guests, you should send printed invitations. Usually the person who is hosting the ceremony and reception issues the invitations. Again the wording of them will depend on your individual situation (examples are given in the chapter on invitations).

Gifts are not expected for a second wedding, though many guests may choose to send one. Accept any gifts graciously and acknowledge them with thank-you notes. It is not correct to indicate "no gifts" on the invitation.

When a large reception follows a small ceremony, a formal reception invitation should be sent to all the guests; simply insert a ceremony card for guests who are invited to both.

THE RECEPTION

The reception may be any size or style you wish. Neither the bride's nor the groom's previous marriages have any effect on this. Having a large reception is a nice way of including friends who couldn't be included in the ceremony.

You may still toast with champagne, cut the wedding cake, and have a "first dance." First wedding customs like tossing the bride's bouquet and garter should be omitted.

REAFFIRMING YOUR WEDDING VOWS

Even if you are about to say your vows for the first time, this may give you an idea of how to reaffirm them in your future years together.

Reaffirming the wedding vows has become more popular in recent years, especially with couples who were married in civil ceremonies or eloped, due to convenience or lack of finances. The renewal of vows may take place shortly after the wedding day, but is more commonly done by couples who were married quite a while ago.

The couple may choose to repeat the same vows they once said, or they may want to write new ones that express the way their love for one another has grown over the years. The ceremony possibilities for a reaffirmation are varied—the ceremony may be small with close friends and family, or larger to include new friends you have acquired over the years. You may choose to have it in a church, or plan it at your home or in a garden. It's a nice idea to make children, if there are any, a part of the ceremony. Many choose to combine it with a special anniversary, such as the tenth or twenty-fifth. Then they have the ceremony first, followed by a festive party.

WAYS TO INCLUDE CHILDREN

Whenever children are involved in a wedding, the engaged couple has to make a decision as to the extent of that involvement. The choices will be determined by the couple's own preferences and the needs of the children. Merging two separate families is not always easy. Depending on how it is handled, it can either be unifying for the couple or it can add increased tension to an already difficult task. It is important to realize that the way the issue of children is dealt with now can influence how successful you may be in merging the two families later.

The most important thing is for you and your fiance to communicate and discuss with each other your feelings and thoughts on the children's role in the wedding. The remarriage of a parent is difficult for most children to accept. To make it as easy as possible for children to adjust to the new situation, you should include them in the wedding plans from the very beginning. They should not merely be told you're getting married, but should be made to feel they are actively involved as participants in the planning, shopping and decision making. Of course, every situation is different. Some children may choose not to become involved, and that's O.K. But what's important is to make them feel very special during this hectic time, when they could easily feel neglected.

If you and your fiancé decide you don't want the children involved in the actual ceremony, there are a number of other ways to include them in the wedding festivities. Finding some way of participating for each child will minimize the fear of being excluded.

Tips for Handling Children

The following are some ideas.

- They should be the first to be told the exciting engagement news. It's best they hear it from you, and not someone else.

- You and your fiance should discuss ahead of time the type and degree of the children's participation with which you're comfortable. Avoid disagreements and hurt feelings.

- Consider including them in the bridal party—as bridesmaids, best man, usher, flower girl or ring bearer.

- Ask for their help in specific areas. Take them shopping and ask their opinions.

- Include the children in a "special ceremony" within the wedding ceremony.

SPECIAL CEREMONIES TO INCORPORATE CHILDREN

Circle of Acceptance

This ceremony is a nice way to incorporate children into the ceremony. The children are called up to the altar. With their parent, the officiant, and new stepparent, they hold hands to form a circle. The officiant says that he realizes the children have had the undivided love and attention of their parent, and that it may be difficult to accept someone else into the family circle. They are reminded that now they have the love and support of both their parent and the new stepparent. He suggests that, in the future, they should reflect back on this moment to help them overcome any difficult times. The officiant then states, "Your parents wish to seek your blessing and support..."; at that moment the children are asked to express their acceptance.

The Family Medallion Ceremony

The Family Medallion is a symbol demonstrating that parents and stepparents intend to be faithful to the children brought together by remarriage. It was created by the Rev. Roger Coleman out of his experience as a clergy person performing wedding ceremonies, often with children present.

The Family Medallion is an attractive necklace given to children during the wedding. This unique symbol has three raised circles on its face. Two circles represent the marriage union, while the third symbolizes the importance of children within the marriage. Because the Family Medallion represents family love in the same way the wedding ring signifies conjugal love, it has become a universal symbol for family relationships.

After the newlyweds exchange vows, the children of both spouses are invited to the altar. During a brief ceremony, the couple places a Family Medallion around the neck of each child, as they pledge to love and support all the children either spouse brings to the marriage. This ceremony, "Celebrating the New Family," is easily adapted to any wedding tradition.

CHAPTER TWENTY

The Rehearsal

The rehearsal is very important and should not be overlooked. It is your insurance that everything is ready and all your attendants are present and informed as to their participation. Generally the rehearsal takes place the night before the ceremony, with a dinner party to follow. However, you may schedule it a couple days in advance if you plan on the party involving a late night or a lot of drinking. Try to schedule the rehearsal so everyone attends, including soloists and organists or instrumentalists. If contemporary songs are being used, possibly a record or tape will do.

It is helpful for everyone if you are able to keep the details as close to the real event as possible, with the exception of wardrobe, flowers and candles, if used. You should still designate where these items will be placed. Rehearsing to the processional music will help attendants measure their steps on the way down the aisle. Remind them not to run down the aisle during the recessional, even though the music is faster. Your clergyman or officiant will help you run through the pace and direct the procedures. If you are unsure of anything, this is the time to ask. When everyone knows exactly what they are to do, the ceremony will run smoothly.

Young attendants can either stand at the altar throughout the ceremony, or join their parents after the processional until the recessional begins. This may depend on the age of the children and the length of the ceremony.

A FINAL NOTE:

Make sure your attendants know their duties and what time they are to be at the ceremony. Ushers should be there at least thirty minutes before the ceremony to seat early arrivals. They should know to seat the bride's family on the left side and the groom's family on the right, and who is seated in the reserved section.

PROCESSIONAL ORDER

Christian or Reformed Jewish

In most cases the clergyman will be standing at the altar, while the groom and best man are positioned in front on the right side. Some traditions have the clergyman precede the groom and best man down the aisle. The processional is then led by the ushers, in order of heigtht, walking in pairs or singly. The bridesmaids follow in a similar arrangement. The maid of honor is next, followed by the ringbearer and flower girl. Finally the bride on her father's arm. In the Christian ceremony your father takes his seat after "giving you away."

Orthodox or Conservative Jewish

The processional order is usually the same for both Orthodox and Conservative ceremonies. The procession is led by the ushers, paired or singly, followed by the best man. Then comes the groom with his father on his left side and mother on his right, followed by the bridesmaids, paired or singly, and then the maid of honor. The ringbearer and flower girl, if any, precede the bride, who walks down the aisle with her father on her left and mother on her right.

RECESSIONAL ORDER

The recessional is led by the joyous newlyweds, immediately followed by the bridal party, the bride's parents, then the groom's parents. The bridal party traditionally walks out in the following order: flower girl and ringbearer together, the best man and maid of honor, the ushers and bridesmaids paired together. Extra ushers or bridesmaids may exit alone.

REHEARSAL DINNER PARTY

This is a nice way to thank your attendants and spend some time with them before the ceremony. You may not get much of a chance to visit with them at the reception. Generally this party is given by the groom's parents. However, anyone can host it, if the parents are some distance away. Another solution is for a friend or relative to plan and organize the party, with the groom's parents paying the bill, or a portion of it.

The guests that should be included are both sets of parents, all the adult attendants of the bridal party with their spouses or dates, and the parents of the child attendants. Small children should be taken home after the rehearsal, to get a good night's sleep so they will be on their best behavior for the wedding. You may also want to include other relatives – grandparents, cousins, aunts, uncles, or out of town guests.

If the party is the night before the ceremony, try to make it an early evening and keep drinking in moderation. You don't want sick or hung-over attendants. You may want to toast both your parents and thank your bridal party, and give them their gifts, if you haven't already done so.

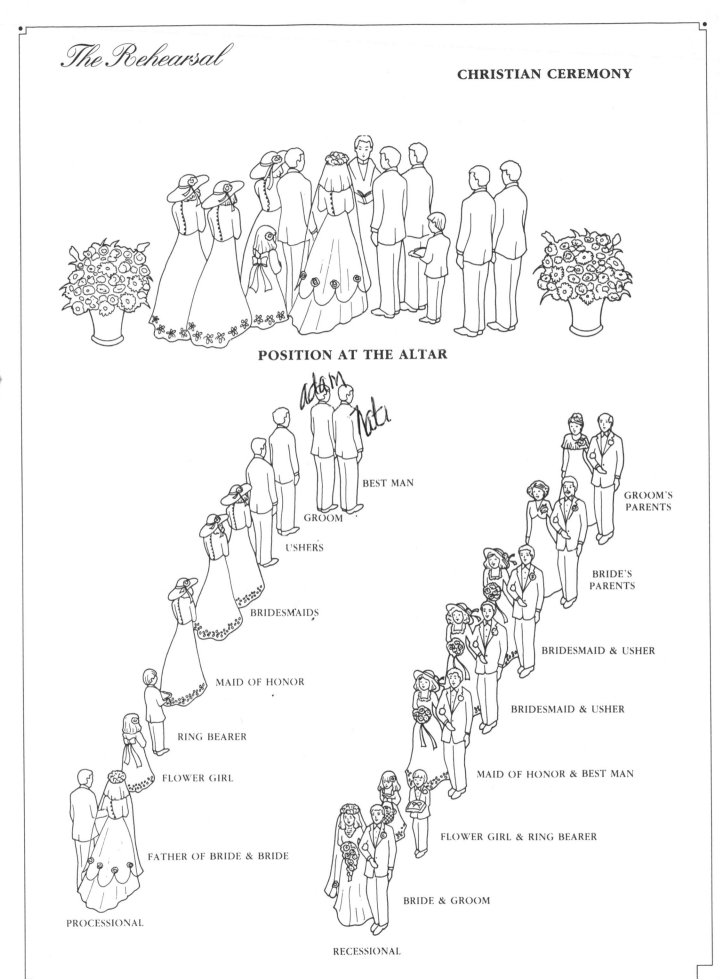

POSITION AT THE ALTAR

BEST MAN

GROOM

USHERS

BRIDESMAIDS

MAID OF HONOR

RING BEARER

FLOWER GIRL

FATHER OF BRIDE & BRIDE

PROCESSIONAL

GROOM'S PARENTS

BRIDE'S PARENTS

BRIDESMAID & USHER

BRIDESMAID & USHER

MAID OF HONOR & BEST MAN

FLOWER GIRL & RING BEARER

BRIDE & GROOM

RECESSIONAL

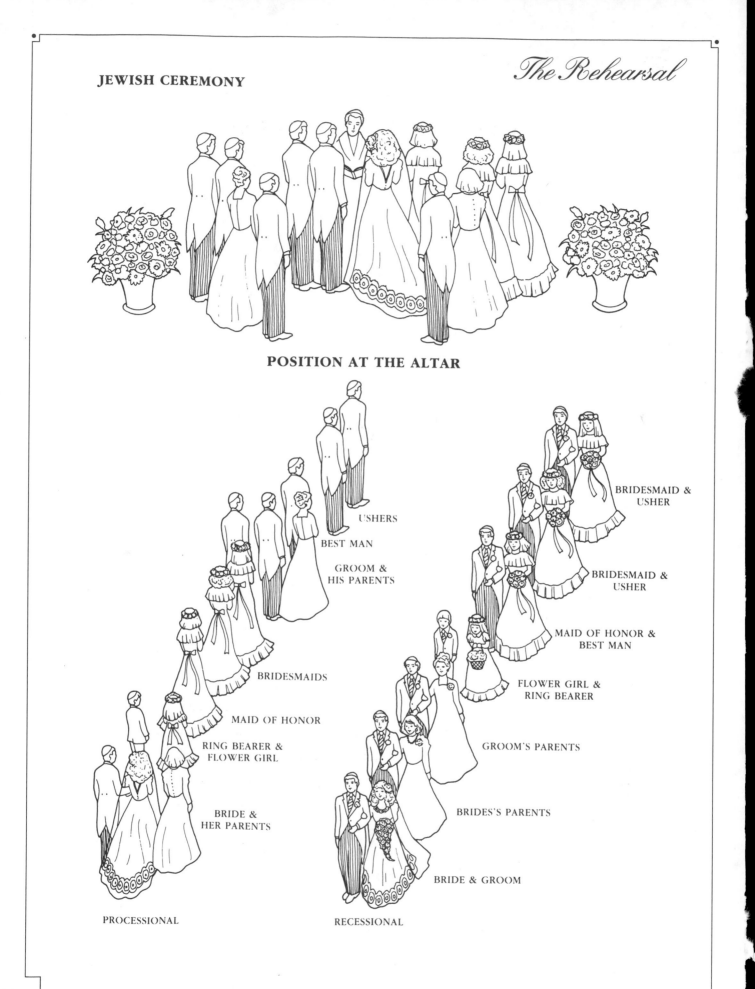

POSITION AT THE ALTAR

USHERS

BEST MAN

GROOM &
HIS PARENTS

BRIDESMAIDS

MAID OF HONOR

RING BEARER &
FLOWER GIRL

BRIDE &
HER PARENTS

PROCESSIONAL

BRIDESMAID &
USHER

BRIDESMAID &
USHER

MAID OF HONOR &
BEST MAN

FLOWER GIRL &
RING BEARER

GROOM'S PARENTS

BRIDE'S PARENTS

BRIDE & GROOM

RECESSIONAL

REHEARSAL PARTY GUEST LIST

Date of Party _____   Location _____

Time _____   Phone _____

	Name	Address, City, Zip	Phone
1.			
2.			
3.			
4.			
5.			
6.			
7.			
8.			
9.			
10.			
11.			
12.			
13.			
14.			
15.			
16.			
17.			
18.			
19.			
20.			
21.			
22.			
23.			
24.			
25.			
26.			
27.			
28.			
29.			
30.			

REHEARSAL CHECKLIST

Rehearsal site _____ Date _____ Time _____

Address _____

Contact Person _____ Phone _____

Rehearsal Dinner site _____ Phone _____

Address _____ Time _____

DON'T FORGET:

	Packed
"Planning a Wedding to Remember"	❏
Attendants' checklist and information	❏
Parents' and helpers' duties and information	❏
Coordinator's checklist	❏
Wedding programs	❏
Maps or written directions	❏
Wedding day transportation information	❏
Practice bouquet	❏
Shoes to be worn	❏
Unity candles	❏
Wine goblets, wine, opener for ceremony	❏
Toasting goblets for reception	❏
Cake knife and server for reception	❏
Guest book and pen	❏
Marriage license	❏
Fee for site rental	❏
Fees for musicians	❏
Fee for officiant	❏
Gifts for helpers	❏
Gifts for attendants	❏

Activities, announcements, comments: _____

_____

_____

CHAPTER TWENTY-ONE

Your Wedding Day

At last, That Special Day! The one you have been spending months planning with anticipation. Don't be at all surprised if you're nervous. That's part of being a bride. It's only a combination of stage fright and excitement. Try to relax and enjoy yourself – the time goes quickly; the day will be over before you know it!

GETTING READY FOR THE CEREMONY

Hopefully, you had a good night's sleep, and with all those months of proper planning and organization, you should have nothing to worry about!

Review the checklist and timetable you should have made a few days in advance. Check off last minute details as they are done. Make sure you have allowed yourself plenty of time for everything, and allow a little extra for unexpected things that may come up. It's a good idea to give copies of the timetable to your bridal party and maybe to your photographer. Make sure he knows when and where you're dressing for your pre-ceremony pictures. Make sure the bouquets and boutonnieres have arrived and that the ushers know their duties and have their list for special seating.

The groom is probably as nervous as you are, and maybe even more so. Don't leave anything to chance. Make sure, along with his and the best man's timetable, you include a checklist reminding them to bring the ring and the license. Add to the list any other duties they may have. It wouldn't be the first time if the wedding was delayed, but this may help to avoid that, providing they don't lose the list.

MAKING IT THROUGH THE CEREMONY

When making your own checklist and timetable, refer to the chapter on the *Wedding Calendar,* which takes you up to the start of the procession. You have probably rehearsed, so everyone knows what to do. Your clergyman or officiant will guide you through the ceremony. If you are reciting a poem,or your own vows to one another, you will be greatly relieved if you have it written on a small paper. It is common to forget your lines when you are nervous. Good luck!

AT THE RECEPTION

Congratulations! Your hands and knees can stop shaking. You've made it through the ceremony, so relax, greet your guests, and enjoy the celebration.

The reception usually starts with a receiving line, a nice way to greet guests and thank them for sharing your special day. If the number of guests is small, you may want to greet them immediately after the ceremony.

When there is a receiving line at the reception, it is best to select the site ahead of time. Choose a location where there is plenty of room for the guests to flow quickly and smoothly to avoid congestion. Keep the conversation short – you don't want guests to have to stand in line too long. This is a good time to get them to sign the guest book; it can be placed either before or after the line.

Your mother usually heads the line, while your father circulates among the guests. The decision of who stands in the line is up to you. However, the best man, ushers, flower girl, and ringbearer normally do not participate. With a larger reception, you may want to eliminate the maid of honor and bridesmaids from the line, to help it move more quickly.

THE RECEIVING LINE

On the following page are some suggestions that may help you prepare your receiving line, and examples of how it may be arranged.

- You and the groom review the guest list with both families to refresh your memory on names.

- Look over both your lists to remember the names of each friend's husband or wife.

- Introduce yourself to guests you don't know.

- If you forget a name – which is easy to do – smile, thank the person for coming, or apologize and ask to be reminded.

- Smile at everyone, shake hands, or give a hug and kiss to those you know better.

- Gloves should not be worn.

- You may have ushers or waitresses bring something to drink for the guests in line.

- Go to the restroom or get a drink, if needed, before forming the line, but do it quickly.

- Arrange for a place to hold the bouquets or for someone to take them.

BRIDE'S MOTHER, FATHER   GROOM'S MOTHER, FATHER   BRIDE & GROOM   MAID OF HONOR

BRIDE'S MOTHER   GROOM'S MOTHER, FATHER   BRIDE & GROOM   MAID OF HONOR, BEST MAN

BRIDE'S MOTHER, FATHER   BRIDE & GROOM   GROOM'S MOTHER

PLANNING YOUR TIME

As with the ceremony, the time goes by quickly, and it's a good idea to make a timetable for yourself, your caterer, musicians and photographer. Of course, this will be just a guideline to help maintain a smooth flow of events, but is especially necessary when you have a time limit on the location.

Most receptions last from three to five hours. Adjust your schedule accordingly. Below is a sample schedule.

First Half-hour:

_____ Wedding pictures are taken, if they weren't before the ceremony. Guests start arriving, mingling, and getting something to drink. Music has begun.

Second Half-hour to Hour-and-a-half.

_____ Receiving line is formed, guests pass through. Guest book is signed, and table cards picked up, if any. Hors d'oeuvres or finger food are passed.

Second Hour

_____ Buffet is announced or guests seated, if you are having a sit down meal. Wedding party is seated and served. Food is served to guests. Best man proposes the first toast.

Third Hour

_____ Any speeches are made by the bride, groom or family. First course is cleared from head table. Bride and groom have the first dance. Guests may follow on the dance floor.

Three-and-a-half Hours.

_____ Tables are cleared. Guests may mingle or dance. Musicians announce cake-cutting ceremony. Cake is cut and served. Dance music resumes.

Last Half-hour

_____ Bride throws bouquet.

_____ Groom throws the garter.

_____ Bride and groom change into going away clothes. Rice, birdseed or dried rose petals are given to guests, if not placed on the table earlier, then tossed on the bride and groom as they run to their car. The bar closes, music stops, and guests start to leave. Parents gather personal belongings and gifts before leaving.

RECEPTION SEATING

Reception seating arrangements can vary, depending on the type and formality of the reception or the layout of the location. It is always best to select a head or centrally located table for the bride's table. After all, it's you they came to see, you should be the center of activity. For a buffet with open seating, be sure to reserve this table; you would not want to embarrass anyone who happened to sit there unknowingly.

The bridal table may include only the parents with the bride and groom, or you may want only the attendants, with or without spouses or dates. A third alternative would be to combine the first two. This decision may depend on several things: the size of the bridal party, the amount of space, the size of the table, and whether the parents are divorced.

The seating arrangements are up to you. However, you may request the help of your mother and the groom's mother when it comes to assigned seating. Try to seat people at a table where they know at least one person, or have similar interests with the others. The other alternative is to let them choose their own seats.

Usually, very formal luncheon or dinner receptions require a seating plan designated by a seating chart or place cards. For formal or semi-formal receptions, place cards are optional, and informal receptions, in most cases, have open seating or standing, depending on the type of reception.

Young children should always be seated with parents. Use your discretion when it comes to teenagers; seat them with parents or place them at a table together.

Unique ideas for a small intimate wedding, or one with a large budget:

• Give each guest a small porcelain bell (like the one on the back cover) with the bride's and groom's name on the outside and the guest's table number painted on the inside. A great memento for them to take home.

• Have each guest's name engraved on a wine or champagne glass and placed on the table as their place card. They must find their own glass before sitting. The glass is something they can take home.

• At a number of specialty chocolate shops, you can have your guests' names carved in chocolate. A big hit with chocolate lovers!

GIFTS BROUGHT TO THE RECEPTION

Some of your guests will bring gifts to the reception. Many hotels and restaurants will take the gifts and look after them for you. A good security system is to have each guest sign his/her name on a list next to a number. That same number is then written on the gift. When you leave, check to see that every gift signed for is there. If the reception is in a home, garden or hall, provide a table for the gifts and have someone keep an eye on them.

In either event, it's a good idea to bring scotch tape. Have the person taking the gifts tape the card securely on each one. Believe me, this extra effort can save hours of trying to figure out who gave you what.

TOASTING

Traditionally, the honor of the first toast is given to the best man. He commands the guests' attention at any time after the receiving line, and after the guests have been served a toasting beverage. He should begin by referring to his relationship with the couple and then proceed to wish them a long and happy life together.

Once the toast is proposed, the guests stand (if seated) holding up their glasses, and then drink to the couple. The traditional beverage for toasting or special celebrations is champagne; however, white wine or punch is often used. The bride and groom do not stand or drink when being toasted.

Other members of the bridal party may want to propose a toast. It is best if the toasting is limited to a few. The groom may then toast his bride, his parents and his new in-laws. Once the toasting is over any congratulatory telegrams are read by the best man.

DANCING

The leader of the band or master of ceremonies should signal the beginning of the dancing formalities. This usually occurs just before, or immediately after, the main course is served. The dance floor should be located near, or in front of, the bride's table. Traditionally, you and the groom lead off the first dance. If the reception is large, with open seating or standing, you may choose to have the guests start dancing after they go through the receiving line. This gives them something to do while you finish greeting guests and catch your breath. The dance floor can then be cleared, and all eyes focused on the bride and groom as they begin their first dance as husband and wife. (You may want to practice a little beforehand.)

Listed below is the order of the traditional dance formality. However, many choose to open the dancing to all after the first dance, which could prevent an uncomfortable situation when divorced parents are involved.

• The first dance is for the bride and groom together, on the dance floor by themselves.

• The bride's father cuts in and dances with his daughter while the groom asks the bride's mother to dance.

• The groom's father cuts in and dances with the bride, while the bride's father cuts in on the groom to dance with his wife.

• The groom then asks his mother to dance.

• The bride dances with the best man and the groom dances with the maid of honor.

• Attendants and guests join in. Don't forget to make time for another dance or two with your husband.

CUTTING THE CAKE

You will want to feature a large or elaborate cake on its own. A round, skirted table is popular and makes for great pictures. The cake should be cut just before dessert, and while the coffee is being offered for a luncheon or dinner reception. For an afternoon tea, or cocktail reception, the cake is usually served after the receiving line and once guests have their drinks.

The band leader or master of ceremonies announces the event. The groom places his right hand over yours and together you cut the first slice. You then offer one another a bite, which signifies a willingness and a pledge to share life together. The bride may then offer a piece of cake to her new in-laws and the groom should do the same, as a thoughtful gesture. The rest of the cake is then cut by a friend or waitress and served to the guests.

TOSSING THE BOUQUET AND GARTER

Just before you change into your going-away clothes to leave, all the single women are gathered in a central location in hopes of catching the bouquet and being the next to marry.

If a prayer book was carried instead of a bouquet, toss the floral decoration or a small, separate bouquet. With large cascading bouquets, many times the bride buys a smaller, "tossing" bouquet, or is given one by her florist. This allows her to preserve the one she carried down the aisle. Make sure, if your going-away flowers are part of your bridal bouquet, to remove them before tossing.

Another fun tradition that may be observed is the tossing of the bride's garter. Like the women, the single men are gathered in hopes of catching the garter, which signifies the next to wed. Be sure your photographer is prepared. You don't want to miss pictures of the bouquet and garter being tossed.

THE GRAND GETAWAY

The last tradition of the ceremony. You and the groom slip away to change. Be quick; you don't want to leave your guests waiting. Say your goodbyes to family and friends. Then depart in the traditional shower of rice, or in its place, bird seed, dried rose petals, or colorful confetti.

A grand get-away is the perfect end to a festive celebration, and a great way to start your future. Choose your style: the traditionally decorated family car, a romantic antique convertible, a horsedrawn carriage, a stately Rolls Royce or chauffeured limousine, or maybe leave them speechless as you float off in a hot air balloon!

The day may have gone quickly – but you will always have "A *Wedding to Remember*," a day no other day will match.

BRIDE'S WEDDING DAY CHECKLIST

Items	*Packed*
Written vows or poem to be presented	❑
Wedding gown	❑
Veil and headpiece	❑
Additional headpiece for reception	❑
Special bra, panties	❑
Special slip	❑
Extra hosiery	❑
Shoes	❑
Gloves	❑
Jewelry	❑
Make-up, perfume	❑
Nail polish and file	❑
Curling iron, curlers	❑
Comb, brush	❑
Hairspray, extra bobby pins	❑
Mirror	❑
Toothbrush, toothpaste, breath mints	❑
Iron or steamer	❑
Garter	❑
Penny or sixpence	❑
Bible, hanky, etc.	❑
Ring pillow	❑
Flower basket (if not being delivered by florist)	❑
Going-away outfit	❑
Going-away undergarments	❑
Going-away shoes and hosiery	❑
Accessories, jewelry, etc.	❑
Wedding night bag (placed in get-away car)	❑
Honeymoon suitcases (placed in get-away car)	❑

GROOM'S WEDDING DAY CHECKLIST

Items	*Packed*
Written vows or poem to be read	❏
Coat	❏
Trousers	❏
Shirt	❏
Vest or cummerbund	❏
Shoes	❏
Socks	❏
Suspenders	❏
Tie	❏
Ascot	❏
Studs and cuff links	❏
Handkerchief	❏
Underwear	❏
Hat	❏
Gloves	❏
Toiletries	❏
Money	❏
Credit cards	❏
Other	❏
Going-away clothes:	
Jacket	❏
Slacks	❏
Shirt	❏
Belt	❏
Tie	❏
Shoes, socks	❏
Accessories	❏
Honeymoon itinerary, tickets, etc.	❏
Wedding night bag (placed in get-away car)	❏
Honeymoon suitcases (placed in get-away car)	❏

CHAPTER TWENTY-TWO

Your Honeymoon

Believe me, you'll need a honeymoon! One thing no one tells you is how tired you can get with all the planning, organizing and emotional tension that builds up to the day of the wedding. With all the friends and relatives around, the two of you probably will have little time to be alone. Whether it be for only a few days or a few weeks, take some time to unwind and enjoy each other. Go somewhere new and exciting! He may want to surprise you, but more often couples plan together.

If you're both involved in the honeymoon planning, start talking as soon as possible. Like everything else, some places are reserved months in advance. By planning and reserving early, you will have a better chance of getting just the accommodations or airline flight you want—and probably at a better price. Determine how much money you have, or will have, to spend, and how long you can be gone. We would all love six months and an unlimited budget, but for most of us this isn't the case. So both of you should talk over the dates and length of time with your employers far in advance. If, for any reason, you are both unable to leave for a lengthy time, try to take a couple of days after the ceremony, and possibly an extended trip later in the year.

YOUR FIRST NIGHT

Many couples decide to spend their first night together in a hideaway honeymoon suite near their reception location, especially when it's an evening wedding. Reserve something special, the bridal suite or a romantic cottage with a fireplace. Tell the manager the occasion, and you may find a bottle of champagne, or breakfast in bed. This gives you time to catch your breath or get together with friends who have come from out of town.

WHERE TO GO

If you don't have a good travel agent, find one. A good travel agent can provide first-hand knowledge that can make final decision-making a lot easier. He/she can recommend the best places to stay. Travel agents are up on the latest and cheapest air fares, and give you tips on things to do, and what to take with you. All you have to decide is where you want to go—they will do the rest.

They can even be helpful with money matters. Discuss with them the amount of money you would like to spend, the length of time you have, and what both of you like and want to do. Perhaps a relaxing week on a secluded beach in Hawaii, or an active week of skiing in the Swiss Alps. You may start by looking through the beautiful color brochures that every travel agency has. Wherever you go, you'll have a great time just being together.

SOME HELPFUL HINTS

• Take most of your money in traveler's checks for security.

• Take national credit cards, if any, for things like car rentals.

• Make a list of all traveler's checks, credit cards and checking account numbers. Take it with you, but keep it in a separate location.

• Label luggage with names, address and phone number on the inside, as well as the outside.

• Make a list of luggage contents. The list will be helpful if needed for claiming any losses.

• Don't forget a camera; have it well labeled.

• Carry with you the names, addresses and phone numbers of your family in the event of an emergency.

• Leave your destination and hotel plans with both families in case they need to reach you.

• Make sure you have homeowner's or renter's insurance that covers your belongings, including all your new gifts. If not, increase your coverage.

• Take your driver's license, marriage certificate and passport or visa, if needed.

COMING HOME TOGETHER

After spending a wonderful honeymoon, it's time to come home and start planning your new life together. As tradition has it, this new life is started with the groom carrying his bride over the threshold of their new home.

Whether you have a simple or elaborate wedding, it will always be a special day in your heart, and one you will always remember.

HONEYMOON ITINERARY

Travel Agency _____

Address _____

Agent _____ Phone _____

Number of days _____ Estimated cost _____

Honeymoon dates: From _____ to _____

Honeymoon destination(s): _____

WEDDING NIGHT

Hotel _____ Phone _____

Address _____

Room accommodations _____ Room# _____

Rate _____ Includes _____ Reservations ❏ Made ❏ Confirmed

TRAVEL RESERVATIONS (airline, ship, train, rental car):

Departure/Pickup		Carrier/Number:	Phone:	Rate:	Arrival/Return		Confirmed
Date:	Time:				Date:	Time:	
_____	_____	_____	_____	_____	_____	_____	❏
_____	_____	_____	_____	_____	_____	_____	❏
_____	_____	_____	_____	_____	_____	_____	❏
_____	_____	_____	_____	_____	_____	_____	❏
_____	_____	_____	_____	_____	_____	_____	❏

HOTEL RESERVATIONS

Arrival date _____ Departure date _____ ❏ Confirmed

Hotel _____ Phone _____

Address _____

Arrival date _____ Departure date _____ ❏ Confirmed

Hotel _____ Phone _____

Address _____

Arrival date _____ Departure date _____ ❏ Confirmed

Hotel _____ Phone _____

Address _____

HONEYMOON CHECKLIST

PAPERS AND DOCUMENTS

Items needed, depending on travel destination	Packed/Have Bride	Packed/Have Groom	Need to Get Bride	Need to Get Groom
Driver's license	❏	❏	❏	❏
Marriage license	❏	❏	❏	❏
Passports	❏	❏	❏	❏
Visas	❏	❏	❏	❏
Copy of birth certificate	❏	❏	❏	❏
Inoculations needed	❏	❏	❏	❏
Copies of Prescriptions	❏	❏	❏	❏
Airline tickets	❏	❏	❏	❏
Other	❏	❏	❏	❏

	Bank	Phone	Have
TRAVELER'S CHECKS	_____	_____	❏

Numbers: _____

_____

CREDIT CARDS (information to be used in the event cards are lost or stolen):

Card Name	Company/Bank	Account Number	Phone	Bride's	Groom's
_____	_____	_____	_____	❏	❏
_____	_____	_____	_____	❏	❏
_____	_____	_____	_____	❏	❏
_____	_____	_____	_____	❏	❏
_____	_____	_____	_____	❏	❏
_____	_____	_____	_____	❏	❏
_____	_____	_____	_____	❏	❏
_____	_____	_____	_____	❏	❏

CHECKING ACCOUNT NUMBERS (In the event checks are lost or stolen):

Name on Account	Bank	Account Number	Phone	Last Check #
_____	_____	_____	_____	_____
_____	_____	_____	_____	_____

DOCTORS (In case of emergency):

	Doctor's Name	Phone	Allergies, medical condition
Bride's	_____	_____	_____
Groom's	_____	_____	_____

CHAPTER TWENTY-THREE

Important Information At A Glance

NAMES, NUMBERS & ACTIVITIES

NAMES AND NUMBERS

FAMILY MEMBERS

_____ _____ - _____
_____ _____ - _____
_____ _____ - _____
_____ _____ - _____
_____ _____ - _____

BRIDAL PARTY & HELPERS

_____ _____ - _____
_____ _____ - _____
_____ _____ - _____
_____ _____ - _____
_____ _____ - _____
_____ _____ - _____
_____ _____ - _____
_____ _____ - _____
_____ _____ - _____
_____ _____ - _____
_____ _____ - _____
_____ _____ - _____
_____ _____ - _____
_____ _____ - _____
_____ _____ - _____
_____ _____ - _____

CEREMONY SITE & OFFICIANT

_____ _____ - _____
_____ _____ - _____
_____ _____ - _____

RECEPTION SITE & CONSULTANT

_____ _____ - _____
_____ _____ - _____
_____ _____ - _____

BRIDAL SALON & FORMALWEAR SHOP

_____ _____ - _____
_____ _____ - _____
_____ _____ - _____

PROFESSIONAL SERVICES

_____ _____ - _____
_____ _____ - _____
_____ _____ - _____
_____ _____ - _____
_____ _____ - _____

PARTY HOSTESSES OR RESTAURANTS

_____ _____ - _____
_____ _____ - _____
_____ _____ - _____
_____ _____ - _____

TRAVEL AGENT, HOTELS, AIRLINES

_____ _____ - _____
_____ _____ - _____
_____ _____ - _____
_____ _____ - _____
_____ _____ - _____

OTHERS

_____ _____ - _____
_____ _____ - _____
_____ _____ - _____
_____ _____ - _____

WEDDING ACTIVITIES

BRIDAL SHOWER:

Date _____ Time _____ Phone _____

Hostess _____ Location _____

Address _____

BRIDAL SHOWER:

Date _____ Time _____ Phone _____

Hostess _____ Location _____

Address _____

BRIDAL LUNCHEON:

Date _____ Time _____ Phone _____

Location _____ Contact person _____

Address _____

CEREMONY REHEARSAL:

Date _____ Time _____ Phone _____

Location _____ Contact person _____

Address _____

REHEARSAL DINNER:

Date _____ Time _____ Phone _____

Location _____ Contact person _____

Address _____

WEDDING CEREMONY:

Date _____ Phone _____

Location _____ Contact person _____

Location to dress _____ Photography time _____

Address _____

OTHER WEDDING ACTIVITIES:

Date	Time	Activity	Location	Phone
_____	_____	_____	_____	_____
_____	_____	_____	_____	_____
_____	_____	_____	_____	_____
_____	_____	_____	_____	_____

Important Information At A Glance

FINAL CHECKLIST

Item & Services	Final Cost	Ordered/Booked
CEREMONY		
Ceremony Site	_____	❏
Officiant	_____	❏
Marriage License	_____	❏
Ceremony Music	_____	❏
Bridal Consultant	_____	❏
Prenuptial Agreement	_____	❏
STATIONERY		
Invitations	_____	❏
Reception cards	_____	❏
Response cards	_____	❏
Announcements	_____	❏
Thank-you notes	_____	❏
Programs/napkins	_____	❏
WEDDING ATTIRE		
Bridal dress	_____	❏
Headpiece/accessories	_____	❏
Groom's formalwear	_____	❏
Bride's attendants	_____	❏
Groom's attendants	_____	❏
Other:	_____	❏
RINGS		
Engagement ring	_____	❏
Bride's wedding ring	_____	❏
Groom's wedding ring	_____	❏
GIFTS		
Gift to bride	_____	❏
Gift to groom	_____	❏
Bridal attendants	_____	❏
Groom's attendants	_____	❏

Item & Services	Final Cost	Ordered/Booked
FLOWERS		
Ceremony flowers	_____	❏
Reception flowers	_____	❏
Bride's flowers	_____	❏
Bridesmaids' flowers	_____	❏
Men's boutonnieres	_____	❏
Mothers'/grandmothers'	_____	❏
RECEPTION		
Reception Site	_____	❏
Caterer	_____	❏
Liquor/beverages	_____	❏
Equipment rentals	_____	❏
Wedding cake	_____	❏
Music	_____	❏
PHOTOGRAPHY		
Formal portrait	_____	❏
Wedding album	_____	❏
Parents' albums	_____	❏
Extra pictures	_____	❏
Videotape	_____	❏
TRANSPORTATION		
Limousines, etc.	_____	❏
Parking attendants	_____	❏
PARTIES		
Bridal luncheon	_____	❏
Bachelor's party	_____	❏
Rehearsal dinner	_____	❏
Other parties:	_____	❏
HONEYMOON		
Hotel accommodations	_____	❏
Travel arrangements	_____	❏